Contents

40. Guinea (Bissau)
41. Gypsy (Romani)
42. Haiti
43. Hebrew
44. Herero
45. Honduran
46. Ice Land
47. Indian
48. Indian (Hindu)
49. Indonesia
50. Iran
51. Irish
52. Italy
53. Jamaica
54. Jewish
55. Kashmiri
56. Kenya
57. Khakas
58. Korean
59. Kurdish
60. Latin
61. Lebanese
62. Liberia
63. Macedonia
64. Malagasy
65. Malaysia (Malay)
66. Manx
67. Maori –New Zealand
68. Mayan
69. Morocco
70. Native American
71. Nepal – Nepalese
72. Netherlands Antilles
73. Niger
74. Nigerian
75. Ovambo
76. Pakistan
77. Palestine
78. Pasho
79. Persian
80. Portuguese

81. Russian
82. Rwanda
83. Sanskrit
84. Scanian
85. Scottish
86. Serbia
87. Somalian
88. Spanish
89. Swahili
90. Syria
91. Tao Sayings
92. Thailand
93. Tunisia
94. Turkey
95. Tywan
96. Uganda
97. Ukraine
98. Vietnam
99. Virgin Islander
100. Walloon
101. Welsh
102. Yiddish
103. Yoddish
104. Zambia
105. Zen
106. Zimbabwe
107. Zimbabwe ((Shona Proverbs)
108. Zulu Proverbs (South Africa)

Background

I have spent seven years researching and writing this book. The quality of this book is amazing. This book is a pool of knowledge, fountain of knowledge. If you seek for wisdom intelligence this the correct book to have. It is verily strongly recommended for Leaders, Pastors, Politicians, Youth seeking wisdom, Parents (imparting knowledge to their children). It can be taught in churches, schools, seminars and any other events.

It is great reference book. It is more than a motivational book. It will guide you, protect you. Knowledge is power and common sense is a shield.

This book will also teach you about different cultures; their style of living, believes and many more. Hope this book will enrich you mentally and that you will grow in knowledge.

Yours with love

Caleb Nathi

Caleb-Nathi

Introduction
This book is a wealth of knowledge. It gives the wisdom of different countries or nationalities. I hope it will be enriching to all who will read it.
It comprise of Proverbs, Maxims, Sayings etc. they are compendium which are commonly confused and misused. The explanation of some of the concepts are explained here under according to Jeff Rovin (Ballantine Books, New York 1994)

Saying / Proverb is the simple, direct term of any pithy expression of or truth. One might comment on sayings of Chairman of Mao or observe that a cynical friend knows the price of everything and as the saying goes.

Proverb is a piece of practical wisdom expressed a homely, concrete terms. For example; a closed mouth catches no flies. Synonymous with an Adage is a short, popular saying that expresses a truth or insight. For example "a word to the wise is sufficient".

An Adage is a saying that has been popularly accepted over a long period of time. For example; where there is smoke there is fire.

An Aphorism is a terse saying that embodies a general, more or less profound truth or principle. For example; "if you came unbidden you depart unthanked". There is more than one way to skin a cat.

An Epigram is a terse, witty pointed statement that often has a clever twist of thought. For example; the only way to get rid of temptation is to yield to it. This is not the same epigraph, which is either an inscription on a monument or building or a brief quotation placed at the beginning of a book or a chapter to suggest its theme.

Maxim is a general principle drawn from practical experience and serving as a rule of conduct. For example; practice what you preach.

Motto is a maxim accepted as guiding principle or as an ideal of behaviour. For example; honesty is the best policy. It's an expression that embodies the philosophy of a person or a group, such as "people are our most important business".

Saw is an old homely saying that is well worn by repetition. For example; "a stitch in time saves nine".

An Apothegm is an edgy more cynical Aphorism, such as "men are generally more careful of the breed of their horses and dogs than of their children.

An Idiom is an expression whose meaning can't be derived simply by hearing it, such as "kick a bucket

PROVERBS

Acholi

1. A crazy man can be recognized not by his words, but by his actions.
2. A dog knows the places he is thrown food.
3. A monkey left behind laughs at the other's tail.
4. Death is a scar that never heals.
5. Each rat with its own whisker.
6. Just because you are poor does not mean you have to sleep with your mother.
7. Old and new millet seeds end up in the same mill.
8. Staying near the anthill turned antelope brown.
9. The first may become the last.
10. The growing millet does not fear the sun.
11. The old pumpkin in the courtyard shall not be uprooted.
12. The one who asks commits no sin.
13. The pot of water falls from your head when you have just reached the door of your homestead.
14. When a lion roars, he does not catch a game.
15. When two elephants fight, it is the grass that suffers.
16. Women have no chief.

Afghan

1. No rose is without thorns.
2. A good year is determined by its spring.
3. Character and quality show up early.
4. Whatever you sow you reap.
5. There is a path to the pot of even the highest mountain.
6. A tree does not move unless there is wind.
7. Don't stop a donkey that isn't yours.
8. There are twenty five uncaught sparrows for a penny.
9. A porcupine speaking to its baby says "o my child of velvet".
10. A wolf's pup will grow into a wolf even though it be raised among men.
11. Flourish like a flower, but may your life be longer.
12. A real friend is one who takes the hand of his friend in times of distress and helplessness.
13. There is a way from heart to heart.
14. The first day you meet, you are friends. The next day you meet, you are brothers.
15. A river is not contaminated by having a dog drink from it.
16. A tilted load won't reach its destination.
17. It's the same donkey but with a new saddle.
18. Without a green switch the ox and the donkey won't obey.
19. Without investigating the water, don't take off your shoes (to walking through it).
20. One flower doesn't bring spring.

21. They asked the fox "who is your witness?" it said "my tail".
22. A lion at home and a fox abroad.
23. A fox is in trouble because of his own pelt.
24. He is riding the donkey but has lost the donkey.
25. In an ant colony dew is a flood.
26. Having been bitten by a snake, be is afraid of a rope.
27. If there is only one bread and onion, still have a happy face.
28. God said "eat and drink" but he didn't say "gorge to the full (up to your throat)".
29. Every anguish passes except the anguish of hunger.
30. A warm fire is better than a delicious food.
31. One, who doesn't appreciate the apple, won't appreciate the orchard.
32. Two watermelons can't be held in one hand.
33. Salt preserve meat, but what can be done with salt if it is bad.
34. A mother won't give milk to her child until she cries.
35. Even if a knife is made of gold, a person won't stab his own heart with it.
36. A new servant can catch a running deer.
37. He ran out from under a leaking roof and sat in the rain.
38. My drum doesn't do what I want it to.
39. Only stretch your foot to the length of your blanket.
40. Walls have mice and mice have ears.
41. Five fingers are brothers but are not equals.

42. A broken hand can work, but a broken heart can't.
43. May God not make one hand depend on the other.
44. Hearing is never as good as seeing (one picture is worth thousands of words).
45. A bad wound heals, but a bad word doesn't.
46. If you sit with us, you will get like us, if you sit beside a cooking pot, you will get black.
47. Not to be considered queer conform to the crowd.
48. Between brother and brother, accounts should be square.
49. One gives by tons, but takes accounts by ounces.
50. No one says his own buttermilk is sour.
51. Give liberally, but do business exactly.
52. Good perfume is known by its scent rather than by the perfumer's advertisement.
53. A poor iron won't make sharp sword.
54. A cheap thinking doesn't lack defect or an expensive thing quality.
55. Vinegar that is free is sweeter than honey.
56. Debt server (is the scissor of) love.
57. Too many butchers spoil the cow.
58. The potter drinks water from a broken jug.
59. Unless God does it, what can a doctor do?
60. Blood cannot be washed out with blood.
61. You can't clap with one hand.
62. Don't be a thief and won't fear the king.
63. Look after your property and you won't accuse your neighbour of being thief.

64. I have never seen anyone go astray who followed along the right way.
65. A liar is forgetful.
66. Under his bowel there is a little bowel.
67. He appreciates prosperity, which is caught in calamity.
68. If a forest catches fire, both the dry and wet will burn up.
69. When water goes over your head, what difference if it's one fathom or a hundred fathoms.
70. Don't sprinkle salt on my wound.
71. Forget the past, but look out in the future.
72. In the ditch where water had flowed, it will flow again.
73. One who runs will also fall.
74. Hasty work doesn't succeed.
75. Patience is bitter, but its fruit is sweet.
76. A river is made drop by drop.
77. He hasn't time even to scratch his head.
78. The seeker is the finder.
79. Smart people get the point from a single hint.
80. Two are better than one, and three than two.
81. A wise enemy is better than a foolish friend.
82. The right answer to a fool is silence.
83. As long as there are fools in the world, no one will be penniless.
84. Ask the truth from a child.
85. Being clean is the half faith.
86. The world lives on hope.
87. Le Christians practice their own religion, and Jews practice theirs.

88. Saying salaam is a sign of true faith.
89. Glory is fitting to God alone.
90. If you don't recognize God, at least know Him by His power.
91. When God gives, He doesn't ask whose son a person is.
92. What my heart desired didn't happen, what God wanted was really done.
93. God isn't need of our prayers.
94. God has said "start moving so that I may start blessing".
95. In childhood you are playful, in youth you are lustful, and in old age you are feeble, so when will you before God be worshipful?
96. Fear the person who doesn't fear God.
97. May Kabu (mountain) be without gold rather than without snow?
98. A lame crab walks straight.
99. Blood will have blood.
100. Bloom where you are planted.
101. Cats don't catch mice to please God.
102. Debts sever love.
103. Don't show me the palm tree, show me the dates.
104. Five (fingers) of them would run from the bang of one empty gun.
105. Give even an onion graciously.
106. If you deal in camels, make doors high.
107. If you want to keep camels, have big enough door.
108. Give every man his due.
109. Storing milk in a sieve, you complain of bad luck.

110. The mud of one country is the medicine of another.
111. The tree will not sway without a trace of wind.
112. What you see in your self is what you see in the world.
113. The wood is burnt, but the ashes are nuisances.
114. What you spend, what you have.
115. When the tiger kills, the jackal profits.
116. Community is not created by force.
117. Little talk, more action.
118. That which thunders do not rain.
119. He who can be killed by sugar should not be killed by poison.
120. He who is cornered will fight.
121. One who calls himself khan is not a khan.
122. What a trumpet job? To blow.
123. When a man is perplexed God is beneficent.
124. He has soaked hundred heads (preparing them for shaving) but hasn't shaved one.
125. W here your heart goes there your feet will go.
126. Where there is discipline there is social order.
127. Don't dig wells for others for you will fall into one yourself.

Algeria

1. A secret for two is soon a secret for nobody.
2. Cross the louder river but don't cross the silent one.
3. Patience is the key to paradise.
4. The one whose belly isn't full of straw isn't afraid of fire.
5. Speak kindly or refrain from talking.
6. Peace wins over wealth.
7. Friendship we call it friendship, but without sincerity.
8. The hand which gives is better than the one that receives.
9. There is an excess of familiarity at the root of all hostility.
10. A friend is someone who shares your happiness and your pains.
11. One hand can't applaud.
12. A sensible enemy is better than a narrow-minded friend.
13. The crow wanted to mimic the pigeon's walk and forgot its own.
14. The one who shows his fears ensures his salvation.
15. When I think of others misfortunes, I forget mine.
16. The absent has always got a justification.
17. You know who your friend and enemy are during difficult moments.
18. Do badly and remember, do well and forget.
19. Who got it, did get it, and who left it, did regret it.
20. As we didn't say a word, he thought he could do anything he liked.

21. Your eye is the only way you can judge things.
22. We taught them to pray, they got the mosque before us.
23. A believer can't be spiteful.
24. The only things left in the Wadi are its stones.
25. Walls have ears.
26. They only fall asleep after having mutually taken an oath and then they betray each other.
27. The soft tongue is sucked by the lioness. That is to say that when you speak kindly, you can tame the great carnivores, the most rebellious people, those who inspire terror.
28. The union of means triumph over the lion- unity is strength.
29. To associate oneself is dangerous move.
30. Is used to say that in a choice the options are all as bad as the others.
31. When he was alive, he looked envious at any dates, when he died; they hung a bunch for him.

American

1. A lean agreement is better than a fat judgment.
2. Never swap horses crossing a stream.
3. A cunning man deals in generalization.
4. The love of money is the root of all evil.
5. Don't measure your neighbour's honesty by your own.
6. If your time ain't come not even a doctor can kill you.
7. There are three things that can destroy a preacher; the glory, the gold, the girls.
8. It is better to save than sorry.
9. It is never too late to mend your ways.
10. Practice what you preach.
11. Easy come easy go.
12. Maternity is a matter of facts, paternity is matter of opinions.
13. The more arguments you win the less friends you have,
14. Love many, trust few and always paddle your own canoe.
15. He who hesitates is lost.
16. When it rains, it pours.
17. A contented mind is a continual feast.
18. A good son makes a good husband.
19. A harvest of peace is produced from seed of contentment.
20. A joy that is shared is a joy made double.
21. A lady is a woman who makes it easy for a man to be a gentleman.
22. Advice is least heeded when most needed.
23. Ambition is putting a ladder against the sky.

24. Arrogance is a kingdom without crown.
25. Character is what you are in the dark.
26. Diligence is the mother of good luck.
27. Diplomacy is the art of letting someone else have your way.
28. Each day provides its own gift.
29. He that lives on hope will die fasting.

Arabian

1. A book is like a garden carried in the pocket.
2. A book that remains shut is but a block.
3. A kind word can attract even the snake from his nest.
4. Little and little collected together become a great deal, the heap in the barn consists of single grain and drop and drop make an inundation.
5. A little bird wants but little nest.
6. A little body doth often harbor a great soul.
7. A little debt makes a debtor, a great one an enemy.
8. A man profits more by the sight of an idiot than by oration of the learned.
9. All mankind is divided into three classes, those that are immovable, those that are movable, and those that move.
10. Beware of one who flatters unduly, he will also censure unjustly.
11. Compete don't envy.
12. Death is black camel which kneels at every man's gate sooner or later you must ride the camel.
13. Diligence is a greater teacher.
14. Do not cut down the tree that gives you shade.
15. Fear not the man who fears God.
16. I am prince and you are a prince, who will lead the donkeys.
17. If begging should be unfortunate be thy lot, knock at the large gate only.
18. If you have much, give of your wealth, if you have little give of your heart.

19. If you stop every time a dog barks, your road will never end.
20. Judge a man by the reputation of his enemies.
21. Judge not of a ship as she lies on the stocks.
22. Know each other as if you were brothers; negotiate deals as if you were strangers to each other.
23. Knowledge acquired as a child is more lasting than engraving on stone.
24. Knowledge is a treasure, but practice is the key to it.
25. No man is as good as physician who has never been seek.
26. One coin in the money-box makes more noise than when it is full.
27. Salt will never be worm-eaten.
28. Search knowledge though be in china,
29. Silence is the best answers to the stupid. The fool has his answer on the tip of his tongue.
30. Singing is the best part of repentance.
31. Sins of omission are seldom fun.
32. The difficult is done at once, the impossible takes a little longer.
33. The hasty and the tardy meet at ferry.
34. The hasty angler loses the fish.
35. The hasty hand catches the frogs for throw fish.
36. Throw a lucky man in the sea, and he will come up with a fish in his mouth.
37. Throw dirt enough, and some will stick.
38. Trust in God, but tie your camel.
39. Trust makes way for treachery.

40. Keep your friends close – hold your enemies closer.
41. A fool may be known by six things; anger without cause, speech without profit, change without progress, inquiry without object, putting trust in a stranger and mistaking foes for friends.
42. Examine what is said, not who speaks.
43. When you heard that a mountain was moved believe it, when you hear that someone changed his character do not believe.
44. The enemy of my enemy is my friend.
45. Marriage is like a besiege castle, those who are on the outside wish to get in, and those who are inside wish to get out.
46. A thousand curses never tore a shirt.
47. A wise man associating with the vicious becomes an idiot; a dog travelling with good men becomes a rational being.
48. All strangers are relations to each other.
49. Better a handful of dry dates and content there with than to own the Gate of Peacocks and be kicked in the eye by broody camel.
50. Better a hundred enemies than outside the house than one inside.
51. If I were to trade in winding sheets, no one would die.
52. If the camel once gets his nose in the tent, his body will follow.
53. If you buy cheap meat, when it boils, you smell what you have saved.
54. Let the sword decide after the stratagem has failed.

55. Nothing but a handful of dust will fill the eyes of men.
56. One is better of seated than standing, lying than seated, asleep than awake and dead than alive.
57. Seek counsel of him who makes you weep and not of him who makes you laugh.
58. The barber learns his trade on the orphan's chin.
59. There are no fans in hell.
60. Think of the going out before you enter.
61. Today it may be a fire, tomorrow it will be ashes.
62. He who sees calamity of other people finds his own calamity light.
63. Do not stand in a place of danger trusting in miracles.
64. He who has health has hope, and he who has hope has everything.
65. He who foretells the future lies, even if tells the truth.
66. A promise is a cloud, fulfilment is rain.
67. When a door opens not your knock, consider your reputation.
68. A secret is like a dove, when it leaves my hand it takes wing.
69. When you have spoken the word, it reigns over you, when it is unspoken you reign over it..
70. The fruit of silence is tranquillity.
71. The willing contemplation of vice is vice.
72. A woman can hide her love for 40 years but her disgust and anger not for one day.
73. Even a one eyed guy will wink at a beautiful woman.
74. A fat woman is blanket for winter.

75. Love sees sharply, hatred even sees more sharp, but jealous sees the sharpest for it is love and hate at the same time.
76. Sad are only those who understand.
77. Every head has its own headaches.
78. Write bad things that are done to you in sand, but write good things that happen to you in of marble.
79. Follow the advice of those who make you cry, never of those who make you laugh.
80. When you shoot at an arrow of truth, dip its point in honey.
81. Death was afraid of him because he had a heart of a lion.
82. The devil tempts all men, but idle man tempts the devil.
83. When danger approaches sing to it.
84. None but mule denies his family.
85. A friend is known when needed.
86. When your son is young discipline him, when he grows older, be a brother to him.
87. Let trouble (evil) alone, and trouble will let you alone.
88. When the wolf comes for the sheep, the dogs go to defecate.
89. An intelligent deaf-mute is better than an ignorant person who can speak.
90. If you conduct yourself properly, fear no one.
91. The last resort is the hot rod.
92. Towards the end of the night you shall hear shrill cries.
93. Have faith in a stone and you will be healed.

94. The son of a son is a dear, the son of a daughter a stranger. The son of you son is yours; the son of your daughter is not.
95. Tire out your body, but not your mind.
96. If you come back from a journey, offer your family (something) though it is only a stone.
97. The tree of silence bears the fruits of peace.

Argentina

1. Children's love is like water in the basket.
2. No woman can make a wise man out of a fool, but every woman can change a wise man into a fool.
3. If you have a tail of straw, then keep away from the fire.
4. A man who develops himself is born twice.
5. A dog that barks all the time gets little attention.
6. Associate with good men and you will be one of them.
7. The one who loves you will make you weep.
8. Tears are words the heart can't express.
9. The love that last the longest is the love that is never returned.
10. One of the hardest thing in life is watching the person you love, love someone else.

Australian

1. The bigger the hat, the smaller the property.
2. A champion team will always beat a team of champions.
3. Where there are Torres Strait Islanders there is a community.
4. Unless you are willing to have a go, fail miserably and have another go, success won't happen.
5. As a leader you must celebrate life, you must celebrate success and paradoxically, you must celebrate heroic failures.
6. All our best heroes are losers.
7. Always back the horse named self-interest, son it'll be the only one trying.
8. As a work of art, it reminds me of a long conversation between two drunks.
9. I've never seen anyone rehabilitated by punishment.
10. The true Assie battler and his wife thrust doggedly onward; starting again, failing again implacably thrusting towards success, for success, even if it is only success of knowing that one has tried to the utmost and never surrendered is the target of every battler.
11. If the section cannot remain here alive, it will remain here dead, but in any case it will remain here, should any man through shell-shock or other cause attempt to surrender, he will remain here dead.
12. It's dead easy to die; it's keeping on living that's hard.

13. You never want an Australian with his back against the wall. You put any 12 blokes together and you'll get a job done, whether it's getting a bogged four –wheel-drive off the beach or standing in front of a cricket wicket and making sure we're in a dominant position. It is the same dog, different leg action so to speak.

14. Not lip service nor obsequious homage to superiors, nor servile observance of forms and customs…..the Australian army is proof that individualism is the best and not the worst foundation upon which to build up collective discipline.

15. May as well be here we are as where we are.

16. A Platypus is a duck designed by a committee.

17. Do you know why I have credibility? Because I don't exudes morality.

18. It's no good crying over spilt milk all we can do is bail up another cow.

19. It is long accepted by missionaries that morality is inversely proportional to the amount of clothing people wore.

20. The twentieth century has been characterizes by three developments of great political importance: the growth of democracy, the growth of corporate power, and the growth of corporate propaganda as a means of protecting corporate power against democracy.

21. Nationalism is both a vital medicine and a dangerous drug.

22. When you play a test cricket you don't give the Englishmen an inch, play it tough, and all the way grind them into the dust.
23. It is better to be defeated on principle than to win on lies.
24. If the guy next to you is swearing like a wharfie he is probably a billionaire, or just conceivably a wharfie.
25. A man of business is one who becomes possessed of other people's money without bringing himself under power of the law.
26. A man may be tough, concentrated successful money-maker and never contribute to his country anything more than a horrible example.
27. The best way to help the poor is not to become one of them.
28. Ordinary people need to lead and not sit there and think that governments are going to spoon feed them.
29. There is nothing so costly to the states as a ruined life.
30. Shoot straight you bastards; don't make a mess of it.
31. The most intense hatreds are between political parties but within them.
32. The difference between a stupid man and a wise one is the stupid man's inability to calculate the consequences of the action. The same goes for the government.
33. Encourage your people to be committed to a project rather than just involved in it. You know the difference between involvement and

commitments don't you? In a meal of bacon and eggs, the chicken is involved, the pig is committed.

34. Australians will never acquire a national identity until individual Australians acquire identities of their own.
35. I admire not idealize.
36. Those who lose dreaming are lost.
37. It's like the axe that's had two new blades and three new handles but otherwise is just as it was when grandfather bought it.
38. The law locks up the man who steals the goose from the common, but leaves the greater criminal loose who steals the common from the goose.
39. If I had a donkey what wouldn't go do you think I'd wallop him oh dear no.
40. Why are people so unkind?
41. Nothing they designed ever gets in the way of a work.
42. Dogs must not steal from frogs.
43. If my lips teach the public that men are made mad by the bad treatment, and if the police are taught that they may exasperate to madness men they persecute and ill treat, my life will not be entirely thrown away.
44. I do not pretend that I have led a blameless life, or that or that one fault justifies another but the public in judging a case like mine should remember that the darkest life may now have a bright side.
45. If you go out for a big night and by some misadventure you end up in a prison cell, you can

count on your best friend to bail you out, but your best mate will be in there besides you.

46. Out in the bush, the tarred road always ends just after the house of the local mayor.

47. There is nothing more Australian than spending time in somebody else's country.

48. A queer country so old that as you walk on and on there's feeling comes over you that you are gone back to Genesis.

49. The dowser mistakes the world for a penitentiary and themselves as the warden.

50. The cricket bat is mightier than the pen and the sword combined.

51. It may be that your sole purpose in life is to serve as a warning to others.

52. We cultivate our land but in a different way from the white man, we endeavoured to live with the land; they seemed to live off it.

53. Some mistakes are too much fun to only make once.

54. A truly happy person is the one who can enjoy the scenery on a detour.

55. Before you criticize someone, you should walk a mile in their shoes. That way, when you criticize them, you're a mile away and have their shoes.

56. Keep your eyes on the sun and you will not see the shadows.

57. Those who lost dreaming are found.

58. The more you know, the less you need.

59. We are all visitors to this time this place, we are just passing through, our purpose here is to

observe, to learn to grow, to love….and then we return home.

60. It is easy to remember your enemies; it's easy to forget your friend.
61. A bad worker blames his tools.
62. One man's meat is another man's poison.
63. God help those who help themselves.
64. Blood is thicker than water.
65. You might as well be hanged for a sheep as for a lamb.
66. No one is deaf as those who would not hear.
67. Half a loaf is better than none.
68. Don't blow your won trumpet.

Austrian

1. A light is still light even though the blind man cannot see it.
2. A blind chicken will often find an ear of corn.
3. An educated woman finds few suitors.
4. A lazy man is the devils handyman.
5. A marriage is a procession in which the cross goes first.
6. Anyone who keeps the ability to see beauty never grows old.
7. Do not allow the Gypsies to lure you out behind the furnace.
8. First bake the strudel then sit down and ponder.
9. God gives the wheat, He doesn't bake the bread.
10. History is constantly teaching but it does not find many pupils.
11. If you owe 10,000 dollars you are a customer to the bank. If you 100 million dollars, the bank is a customer yours.
12. If you shoot your arrows at stones, you will damage them.
13. Imitate the sundia's ways count only the pleasant days.
14. Nothing ventured, nothing gained.
15. Old men and poodies are good for nothing.
16. Success has more than one father.
17. The cripple is always the one to open the dancing.
18. The earth does not shake when the flea coughs.
19. The hunt is like a dance for men, for women the dance is the hunt.
20. The most dangerous food is wedding cake.
21. The situation is hopeless, but not serious.

22. There are more chains than mad dogs.
23. There's only one pretty child in the world and every mother has it.
24. To be drunk every day is also regular life.
25. What I do not know will not keep me warm.

Azerbaijani

1. Intelligence is in the head, not in the age.
2. Tree would bend when it bears fruit.
3. Wise enemy is better than a foolish friend.
4. Shame is not the one doesn't know, but the one who doesn't ask.
5. Without sowing single wheat you would not harvest thousand ones.
6. Smart birds get trapped in its beak.
7. Drop by drop would make a lake.
8. Tongue may muddle up and say the truth.
9. Politeness is not sold in the bazaar.
10. Mouth will not be sweet when you say "sweet".
11. Unearned riches are unlawful or forbidden.
12. Every tree casts shadow on its bottom.
13. Someone's end is someone's beginning.
14. A man would not lick what he spit.
15. Dog has to have its stomach full.
16. Forest always has its jackal.
17. Mollah is a human, if an oak will produce an almond.
18. Grass grows on its roots.
19. Bless the builders damn the slayers.
20. Look at my colour (face), know my mood.
21. To tell the dog to catch and the rabbit to run.
22. Those who get up marry early, achieve success.
23. A mad man drops a rock into water well, so that thousand wise men cannot take it.
24. Beauty without virtue is a curse.
25. One's own simple bread is much better than someone else's pilaf.

26. Speak not of what you have read, but about what you have understood.
27. Until spring comes nightingale do not sing.

Bengali (Bangladesh)

1. Half truth is more dangerous than falsehood.
2. While it is the happy time of the Harvest for one, it is complete devastation for someone else.
3. Since the Brahim who owns the land is away, the hired ploughmen stop working.
4. The boat of affection ascends even mountains.
5. Eyes are the mirror of the mind.
6. A one eyed uncle is better than no uncle at all.
7. You may cover a fish with spinach, but can't hide its smell.
8. Time flows like flow of water in a river.
9. You cannot eat a friend fish by flipping it.
10. The deer has enemies because of its flesh.
11. Too much courtesy full of craft.
12. Cut you coat according to your cloth.
13. Too many cooks spoil the broth.
14. To cry in the wilderness.
15. Money is the root of all evil.

Belgium

1. The horse must graze where it is tethered.
2. The beautiful is less what one sees than what one dreams.
3. He who does not wish for little things does not deserve big things.
4. Who sieves too much keeps the rubbish.
5. Weeds never perish.

Bhutanese

1. Don't put an easy tongue in an easy mouth.
2. If the thought is good (your) place and path are good, if the thought is bad (your) place and path are bad.
3. The stripes of a tiger are on the outside, the stripes (character) of a person are on the inside (character is not directly visible)
4. A trustworthy person steals one's heart.
5. Do not start your worldly life too late; do not start your religious life too early.
6. A girl with a dedicated heart and good behaviour is more precious than your own heart.
7. To give happiness to another person give such a great merit, it cannot even be carried by an elephant.
8. Where there is plenty of water, it rains, where there is abundant of heat, the sun shines.
9. Whatever joy you seek it can be achieve by yourself, whatever misery you seek, it can be found by yourself.
10. The rain falls yonder but the drops strike here (the indirect remarks hit the target).
11. On the battlefield, there is no distinction between the upper and lower class.
12. If there is no financial involvement between relatives, the relationship is harmonious.
13. The way the arrow hits the target is more essential than the way it is shot (the way you listen is more essential than the way you talk).
14. Fun and pleasure are located below the navel; dispute and trouble are also located there.

15. Flattering words will not be spoken from the mouth of an affectionate person.
16. Never reveal all that you know to others, they might come shrewder than you.
17. If they don't exchange few words, father and son will never know each other.
18. If you tell the truth, people are not happy, if beaten with stick, dogs are not happy.
19. When there are too many carpenters, the door cannot be erected.
20. In my homeland I possess one hundred horses, yet if I go, I go on foot.
21. To know your limitation is the hallmark of a wise person.
22. If heat is applied to water long enough it will freeze.
23. Walking slowly, even the donkey will reach Lhasa (given determination, even a dolt will eventually reach the goal).
24. The nose didn't smell the rooting head (one can't see one's own faults).
25. One could not cross a bridge constructed by oneself.
26. The arrow of the accomplished master will not be seen when it is realized, only when it hits the target (you don't see the process but the results).
27. A fire should be subdued while young.
28. Consider the tune, not the voice, consider the words not the tune, and consider the meaning, not the words.
29. No death without reason.

30. Words coming from far away are always half true, half false.
31. You must first wall around a bit before you can understand the distance from the valley to the mountain.
32. Clear the drain before it rains.
33. Although the pruce tree is huge, it is hollow inside. The rhododendron, though small blossoms.
34. There is no person without faults; there is no tree without knots.

Botswana (Batswana)

1. Eating without sharing is like swearing with your mouth.
2. To give away is to make provision for the future.
3. We are people because of other people.
4. He who offends forgets, but he who suffered from the offence does not.
5. Eyes can see widely, they cross the river in full flood.
6. Plenty is like the mist.
7. Famine hides under the granary.
8. The cripple is fair in its mother's eyes.
9. To travel is to see.
10. You can't keep a bull in the kraal.

Bulgarian

1. Hasty work – shame for the craftsman.
2. The hasty bitch bears blind one.
3. Every frog must know its pond.
4. In a dispute both sides have been satisfied.
5. It can't be that the wolf is full and the lamb is alive.
6. A hungry bear doesn't dance.
7. You can't find stupidity in the forest.
8. Take a big bite, big words don't say.
9. A crow's eye doesn't peck.
10. The guilty man flees unchased.
11. If you had been calm, you wouldn't have seen a miracle.
12. One swallow doesn't make a spring.
13. Talk of the devil and the devil will appear.
14. Tell me who your friends are, so I can tell you who you are.
15. As you sow you shall reap.
16. Drop by drop a whole lake becomes.
17. He who digs someone else's grave shall fall in it himself.
18. The one who does not work must not eat.
19. The one who sings, evil does not think.
20. He who pulls out a knife, by knife shall die.
21. The one who laugh last, laugh best.
22. The pear does not fall far from there tree.
23. Blood is thicker than water.
24. When the cart rolled over, there are many roads.
25. The wolf has a thick neck because he does not work on his own.
26. A lie's legs are short.

27. A lie has no legs.
28. Don't leave today's work for tomorrow.
29. Beauty, by force is not created.
30. Don't cry at somebody else's grave.
31. He's not crazy; he who eats the pastry, crazy is the one who gave it to him.
32. Out of side out of mind.
33. Help yourself to help God help you.
34. A pot calling cattle black.
35. First impression is from your dress, last impression from your brains / wit.
36. May God help us when the blind ones gains sight.
37. There is no flock without carrion.
38. Measure thrice, cut once.
39. Mind reigns, mind obeys, mind feed the duck.
40. The nice apples are always eaten by nasty pigs.
41. Feed the dog to bark at you.
42. The grass is always greener on other side.
43. Men propose God dispose.
44. A gentle word opens an iron gate.
45. God promises a safe landing but not a calm passage.
46. If you call one wolf, you invite the pack.
47. If you can't be good, be careful.
48. If you can't beat them join them.
49. If you let everyone walk over you, you become a carpet.
50. If you wish to drown, do not torture yourself with shallow water.
51. If you can kiss the mistress, never kiss the maid.
52. Seize opportunity by the beard, for it is bald behind.

53. When the sea turned into honey, the poor man lost his spoon.
54. You are permitted in times of great danger to walk with the devil until you have crossed the bridge.
55. Whatever one does, one does it to oneself.
56. He who thinks evil find evil.
57. Once you have been bitten by a snake you are afraid of even a lizard.
58. A tree is bent while it is slender.
59. A well fed person doesn't believe the hungry person.
60. Big clouds little rain.
61. If the hand gives but the heart doesn't, nothing will come of it.
62. If you cannot serve, you cannot rule.
63. Dip your tongue in wisdom, and then give counsel.
64. Pretty wife, old wine – many friends.
65. A tree fall the way it leans.
66. Nature, time and patience are three great physicians.

Burma (Burmanese)

1. Regret always comes later.
2. Wise man's anger never comes out.
3. Snake to snake, see the leg (snakes have no legs, but crooks can see how other crooks will do)
4. Mango among fruit, pork among meat, tea among leaves (are the best).
5. You can stop speaking to someone, but you cannot stop being related.
6. Do use a needle in time, or you might need an axe later.
7. Collect water while it rains.
8. You can even be a God if you try.
9. You can be a king, if you are brave.
10. Old cows like young grass.
11. Anyone can fancy his bed as a place (you can believe what you want).
12. There's only two ways: go crazy or go extraordinary! (Be somebody).
13. Don't be a sling bag.
14. You can pull back your legs, but not your committed word.
15. It's dress in a man binding in basket edge.
16. Bone in chicken, relatives in man (that one can avoid).
17. Calling out for mother, only when you stumble.
18. Before bending arm straighten, or before the straighten arm bends (do the good, choose better).
19. Be delighted when there's time.
20. Harrow before the cow (instead of the cow before the harrow).

21. Forgetting the cow when going to plough?
22. Fidelity is the king, promise in men.
23. Using up the arrows before getting into the battle.
24. Too many become enemies, when their ideas are the same.
25. If there are too many teachers or leaders with different ideas, the follower will not do nothing and learning nothing.
26. An unmarried woman is not honoured even if she has brothers.
27. Wisdom is in the books (find them there).
28. A ship load of fish gets spoiled because of one spoiled fish.
29. One can't die if he is brave, even when he dies his name last forever.
30. You fail if you are afraid, or brave, you may become a king.
31. A genuine ruby won't sink and disappear in mud.
32. Fisherman near fisherman. Hunter near hunter.
33. Unmistakable lawyer. Immortal medicine man.
34. Seek wisdom like a beggar.

Burma (Loka Niti – words of the wise)

1. Never think of knowledge and wisdom as little. Seek it and store in the mind. Note that ant-hills are built with small particles of dust and incessantly – falling rain drops when collected can fill a big pot.

2. There is no ruby in every mountain. There is no pearl in every elephant. There is no sandal-wood in every forest. There is no sage in every place.

3. One with scanty knowledge tends to think a little learning a lot and be haughty. It is just a puny frog not having seen the ocean, thinks a little well-water a lot.

4. One without learning has to carry others burden. One who has knowledge is honoured by others, so strive daily to get knowledge.

5. As the regret is ungraceful among Hamsas, so also the foolish in an assembly.

6. Listening and nothing well enriches knowledge. Knowledge enhances progress.

7. There is no friend like learning. There is no enemy like disease.

8. Go not! To the battlefield without arm. Speak not without reference to treatise. Travel not afar without companion.

9. Without wealth, be not excessive in eating. Without strength, love not fighting. Without learning speak not too much.

10. Do not visit another's house frequently without being invited. Don't talk too much without being asked. Don't be extol and boast of oneself (don't blow one's trumpet).

11. The pot not full of water is turbulent. One with little knowledge shows off.

12. The ocean is not content in receiving water. The eye is not content in seeing the beloved. The wise is not contented in good speech.

13. Though fully endowed with good looks and youthfulness, he who has knowledge is ungraceful. It is like Paukpwint (pauk flower) without scent.

14. Even the son of low parentage can be the king's counsellor the son of a poor man can be rich, so don't be contemptuous of a man.

15. The pupil who wants knowledge and studies many cannot retell the dream.

16. Pauk leaf that wrap Taungzalat flower smells fragrant like that flower, so also is the same for those who associate with the wise.

Cameroon

1. A chattering bird builds no nest.
2. A cherry year, merry year, a plum year, a dump year.
3. By trying often, the monkey learns to jump from the tree.
4. He who asks questions cannot avoid the answer.
5. Rain does not fall on one roof alone.
6. The elephant will reach to the roof of the house.
7. The heart of the wise man lays quest like limpid water.
8. Thought breaks the heart.
9. Knowledge is better than riches.
10. Water always finds a way out.
11. The cricket cries, the year changes.
12. Do not step on the dog's tail and it will not bite you.
13. Better a mistake at the beginning than at the end.

Catalan – North America

1. For love of the ox the wolf licks the York.
2. He who hunts after bargains will scratch his head.
3. He who waits for another platter has a cold meal.
4. Love does much, Money does all.
5. Secrets fire is discovered by its smoke.
6. Who is tender in everything is a fool in everything.
7. Little by little you fill the sink and drop by drop you fill the barrel.
8. The remedy is worse than disease.
9. To buy cheap is to buy twice.
10. Year of snow, year of God.
11. In a shut mouth, no fly will go in.
12. You will catch a liar first and then you will catch a lame.

Chad (Teda Tribe)

1. If you don't want you contemporary to get ahead give him a loan.
2. One who eats the ear will not rest without eating the eye.
3. When we slit the throat improperly, it's important to skin it properly.
4. The king like the sun will appear one day.
5. One cannot hide on a camel, and one cannot conceal one's footprints in the sand.
6. If you don't consider the relative of your relative as your relative, you cannot be saved (helped).
7. When your mouth learns certain words, a concussion will rise.
8. There is no one who has ten fingers who does not have ten relatives.
9. When a girl is fertile, even the head of the family cannot refuse her bringing into the world a child.
10. A matter and a container have beginning.
11. There is no such thing as small fire or small woman.
12. To the one who does not support you in speech, don't give him a word, to the one who does not watch out for you, don't confide in him.
13. Precaution is not fear.
14. An eye does not kill a gazelle; saliva does not break a fast.

Chad (Sara Tribe)
1. The maternal uncle of a child is the mother of the child.
2. If you respect your friend, you will build the village (at a relational level).
3. Listen to what is said of your friend, listen for yourself also.
4. First the child goes on a trip, and then he discovers the stranger.
5. Death is as the games of "Mende" if your friend plays, play with him.
6. It can stop raining, but hunger has no hunger.
7. The eyes are afraid but the hands are the ones that work.
8. The one who reminds the mouth of the sauce would not dare to drink the sauce down.
9. The things that are on the neck or at the throat do not do them forcefully.
10. The word of the night is the tail of the black margouilla (lizard).
11. If you see what is on your head, what is in your hand will fail.
12. The one who does not climb the tree eats the fruit that is unripe.
13. The monkey who sleeps does not eat the beans.
14. Your neighbour `is the one who kills (extinguishes) the fire at your home.
15. Even the little squash has its seeds.

Chili

1. Whoever eats chilli gets burned.
2. Hear from the right ear, out from the left ear.
3. Like a candle, burning itself to light the people.
4. To bend a bamboo, while it's still shot.
5. Lose when you buy, win when you wear.
6. If you speak in daytime, look around; if you speak at night listen carefully.
7. Fish glisten in the water and it is already clear whether they are male or female.
8. Dare because you are in the right, fear because you are in the wrong.
9. If it is heavy, we carry it together on our shoulders; if it is light we carry it together in our hands.
10. Clapping with one hand will not make a noise.
11. Let it be slow as long as it's safe, a mountain won't run if you chase it.
12. If your fishing line is only a hand span long, don't try to measure how deep the see is.
13. The lot of coconut husk is to float; the lot of stone is to sink.

Chinese

1. A man must insult himself before others will.
2. When anger arises, think of the consequences.
3. Virtue cannot live in solitude, neighbours are sure to grow up around it.
4. Talk does not cook rice.
5. They who know the truth are not equal to those who love it, and they who love it are not equal to those who find pleasure in it.
6. If you walk on a snow you cannot hide your footprints.
7. When the ear will not listen, let heart escape sorrow.
8. The daughter of a crab does not give birth to a bird.
9. Go home and make a net if you desire to get fishes.
10. The journey of a thousand mile start with a single step.
11. Words are the voice of the heart.
12. A vacant mind is open to all suggestion as hollow building echoes all sounds.
13. It takes a little effort to watch a man carry a load.
14. Much wealth will not come if a little does not go.
15. You cannot push a cow's head down unless it is drinking water by its own.
16. The arrogant army will lose the battle for sure.

17. Ten of thousand bones will become ashes when one general achieves his fame.
18. If you are in hurry you will never get there.
19. Use attack as a tactic of defence.
20. Set yourself as the standard.
21. When you have musk, you will automatically have fragrance.
22. You cannot fight a fire with water from far away.
23. Paper cannot wrap up fire.
24. Men should worry about fame just as pigs being fat.
25. Even the most resourceful house wife cannot create a miracle from rice less pantry.
26. The participant's perspectives are clouded while the by stander's views are clear.
27. Pick the flower when it is ready to be picked.
28. If you don't go into the cave of the tiger, how are you going to get its cub?
29. Follow the local custom when you got to a foreign place.
30. It's impossible to change your basic characteristics.
31. Once bitten by snake, you are even frightened by a rope that resembles a snake.
32. Your neighbour's wife looks prettier than your own.
33. When you go up the mountain too often you will eventually encounter the tiger.
34. Elephant's tusk cannot grow out of a dog's mouth.

35. When the tiger comes down from the mountain to the plain, it is bullied by dogs.
36. Water can float a boat and capsize it as well.
37. Diligence is priceless, treasure, prudence is protective charm.
38. Undergo self-imposed hardships to harden one's resolve.
39. Whoever started the trouble should end it.
40. Men who run in front of car get tired.
41. Men who run behind the car get exhausted.
42. Learning is a treasure that will follow its owner everywhere.
43. Man who waits for the roast duck to fly into mouth must wait very, very long time.
44. Medicine can only cure curable disease, and then not always.
45. Add legs to the snake after you have finished drawing it.
46. After three days without reading, talk becomes flavourless.
47. An ant may as well destroy the whole dam.
48. Better do a good deed near home than go far away to burn incense.
49. A book holds a house of gold.
50. Butcher the donkey after it finished his job on the mill.
51. Clear conscience never fears midnight knocking.
52. A closed mind is a closed book, just a block of wood.
53. A dish of carrot hastily cooked may still have soil uncleaned off the vegetable.

54. Dismantle the bridge shortly after crossing it.
55. Distant water won't help put out fire close at hand.
56. Distant water won't quench your immediate thirst.
57. Do not what others to know what you have done better not have it anyways.
58. Donkey's slips do not fit into a horse's mouth.
59. A dog won't forsake his master because of his poverty, a son never desert his mother for her homely appearance.
60. Dream different dreams while on the same bed.
61. The soldier who treated 50 paces jeered at the one who retreated 100 paces.
62. Good luck seldom come in pairs but bad things never walk (occur) alone.
63. Fight poison with poison.
64. Tiger father begets tiger son.
65. Man's schemes are in inferior to those made in heaven.
66. If you have money you can make the ghosts and devils turn grind stone.
67. You want your horse to look good but also want it not to have to eat grass.
68. There is no wave without wind.
69. Parents who are afraid to put their foot down usually have children who step on their toes.
70. A diamond with a flaw is better than a common stone that is perfect.

71. To attract good fortune, spend a new penny on an old friend, share an old pleasure with a new friend and lift up the heart of a true friend by writing his name on the wings of a dragon.
72. If you must play, decide on three things at the start, the rules of the game, the rules of the game, the stakes and the quitting time
73. Habits are cobweb at first, cables at last.
74. A thorn defended the rose, harming only those who would steal the blossom.
75. If I keep a green bough in my heart, then the singing bird will come.
76. Heaven has a road, but no one travels it, Hell has no gate but men will dig to get there.
77. Look for a thing until you find it and you will not lose your labour.
78. He who treads softly goes far.
79. A single conversation with a wise man is worth a month's study of books.
80. The one who pursue revenge should dig two graves.
81. If we don't change our direction, we are likely to end up where we are headed.
82. I hear and I forget, I see and I remember, I do and I understand.
83. Do not anxiously hope for that which is not yet to come, do not vainly regret what is ready past.
84. If you plan for one year, plant rice, if you plan for ten years, plant trees, if you plan for hundred years educate mankind.

85. Outside noisy, inside empty.
86. The journey is the reward.
87. In the midst of great joy, don't promise anyone anything. In the midst of great anger do not answer anyone's letter.
88. One joy scatters a hundred of grief.
89. If you have made him, earth can find some use for him.
90. If you are patient in one moment of anger, you will escape a hundred days of sorrow.
91. If you bow at all, bow low.
92. If you don't want anyone to know don't do it.
93. Not until just before dawn do people sleep best, not until people get old do they become wise.
94. Raise your sail one foot and you get ten feet of wind.
95. Teachers' open door, you enter by yourself.
96. The palest ink is better than the strongest memory.
97. To know the road ahead, ask those coming back.
98. When you drink the water, remember the spring.
99. When you have only two pennies left in the world, buy a loaf of bread with one and a lily with the other.
100. Keep your broken arm inside your sleeves.
101. Behind every able man, there are always able men.
102. If your strength is small, don't carry heavy burdens.

103. If your words are worthless, don't give advice.
104. Men grow old, pearls grow yellow, and there is no cure for it.
105. The woman who tells her age is either too young have anything to lose or too old to have anything to gain.
106. Of all thirty six alternatives, running away is the best.
107. He who sacrifices his conscience to ambition burns a picture to obtain the ashes.
108. He who cannot agree with his enemies is controlled by them.
109. You cannot prevent the birds of sorrow from flying over your head, but you can prevent them from building nest in your hair.
110. A great fortune depends on luck, a small one on diligence.
111. Who is not satisfied with himself will grow, who is not sure of his own correctness will learn many things.
112. To believe in one's dream is to spend all one's life asleep.
113. Heaven lent you a soul, Earth will lend a grave.
114. In a broken nest there are few whole eggs.
115. Wealth or peace, Grievance or safety with too much wealth will always fear being robbed.

116. A bird does not sing because it has an answer, it sings because it has a song.
117. A bit of fragrance (lining to the hand that give flower).
118. A book holds a house of gold.
119. A book is garden carried in the pocket.
120. A book tightly shut is but a block of paper.
121. A child's life is like a piece of paper on which every person leaves a mark.
122. A diamond with a flaw is worth more than a pebble without imperfection.
123. A filthy mouth will not utter decent language.
124. A fool judges people by the presents they give him.
125. A gem is not polished without rubbing, nor a man perfected without trials.
126. A nation's treasure is in its scholars.
127. A rat gnaws at the cat's tail invites destruction.
128. Be no be afraid of growing slowly, be afraid of only standing still (Do not fear going forward slowly, fear only to stand still).
129. Be the first to the field and the last to the couch.
130. Deep doubt, deep wisdom, small doubt small wisdom.
131. Dig the well before you are thirsty.
132. Do good, reap goo, do evil, reap evil.
133. Do not empty handsome servants.
134. Do not remove a fly from your friend's forehead with a hatchet.

135. Don't open a shop unless you like to smile.
136. Each generation will reap what the former generation has sown.
137. Give man a fish and you feed him for a day. Teach a man to fish and you feed him for a lifetime.
138. He who asks is a fool for five minutes, but he who does not ask remains a fool forever.
139. He who is drowned is not troubled by the rain.
140. He who strikes the first blow admits he's lost the argument.
141. One's good deeds are only known at home and one's bad deed far away.
142. A needle is sharp only at one end.
143. Those who know when they have enough are rich.
144. Rotten wood cannot be carved.
145. He who rides a tiger is afraid to dismount.
146. To be a woman means to submit.
147. A woman gets thirty percent of beauty from nature and seventy percent from make-up.
148. It is the beautiful bird which get cage.
149. Study without reflection is waste of time, reflection without study is dangerous – Confucius.
150. Good words are like a string of pearl.
151. A man who has committed a mistake and does not correct it is committing another mistake.

152. When your house is on the brink of precipice it is too late to pull the reins.
153. Everything has it beauty but not everyone sees it.
154. Fool me once, shame on you; fool me twice, shame on me.
155.

Congo

1. A cat goes to a monastery, but she still remains a cat.
2. A pretty basket does not prevent worries.
3. A pretty face and fine clothes do not make a character.
4. A priest sees people at their best, a lawyer at their worst, but a doctor sees them as they really are.
5. Death does not sound a trumpet.
6. Little by little grow bananas.
7. Lower your head modesty while passing and you will harvest bananas.
8. No matter how full the river, it still wants to grow.
9. No matter how hard you throw a dead fish in the water, it still won't swim.
10. What is said over the dead lion's body could not be said to it alive.
11. When the bees come to your house, let her have beer, you may want to visit the bee's house someday.
12. The bald headed man will not grow hair by getting excited.
13. A house with two keys is worth nothing.
14. A little subtleness is better than a lot of force.
15. A single bracelet does not jingle.
16. An idiot will cross an ox with an elephant.
17. Being well dressed does not prevent one from being poor.
18. Children are reward of life.

19. Do not dispose of the monkey's tail before it is dead.
20. Don't buy a boat that is under water.
21. Don't the salt if you haven't licked it yet.
22. Drink beer, think beer.
23. Friendship does not need pepper to cry.
24. Great events may steam from words of no importance.
25. He who does not like chattering women must stay a bachelor.
26. He, who is free of faults, will never die.
27. I owe a cow in heaven, but I cannot drink its milk.
28. If you are too modest you will not go hungry.
29. If you tell people to live together, you tell them to quarrel.
30. Let him speak who has with his eyes.
31. Love is like a baby, it needs to be treated tenderly.
32. Loves do not hide their nakedness.
33. Man is like a palm-wine, when young, sweet but without strength, in old age, strong but harsh.
34. Mothers – in laws are hard of hearing.
35. No matter how full the river, it wants to swell more.
36. No matter how long the night, the day is sure to come.
37. One day of hunger is not starvation.
38. One knife will not cut another knife; one cheat will cheat another cheat.
39. Prepare yourself for when water comes up to your knees.
40. Pride goes only as far as one can split.

41. Sleep is the cousin of death.
42. The absent are always in the wrong.
43. The flesh of young animal tastes flat.
44. The fly has no pity for thin man.
45. The important man does not eat spicy food.
46. The iron never takes advice from the hammer.
47. The mother in law shows you her thighs without shame, you are the embarrassed one.
48. The nuts from the palm tree don't fall without dragging a few leaves with it.
49. The portion that a man keeps for himself is usually not the smallest.
50. The snake and the crab don't sleep in the same hole.
51. The son shoots a leopard, the father is proud.
52. The teeth are smiling, but are the heart?
53. The watched chicken never lays.
54. The white man never forgets Europe.
55. The worm that gnaws on the bean is one inside the bean.
56. Those who inherit fortunes are frequently more of a problem than those who made them.
57. To love someone who does not love you, is like shaking a tree make the dew drops fall.
58. Two birds disputed about a kernel, when a third swooped down and carried it off.
59. War ends nothing.
60. Who sits down is a cripple.
61. Without war there can be no peace.
62. Woe the high spirited bride whose mother in law is still alive.

63. Wood may remain ten years in the water, but it will never become a crocodile.
64. You do not teach the path of the forest to an old gorilla.
65. You inherit from the dead, not from the sick.

Corsican

1. Lies have twisted limbs.
2. A closed mouth catches neither flies nor food.
3. What goes around comes around.
4. The doctor comes to the house where the sun can't reach.
5. Don't look at a gift horse in the mouth.
6. Anyone who lives will know trying times.
7. He who sleeps cannot catch a fish.
8. A fortune teller would never be unhappy.
9. He who puts off something will lose it.
10. When you have been heard you go home.
11. He who leads an immoral life dies an immoral death.
12. He who eats holy bread has to deserve it.
13. He who studies does not waste his time.
14. He who has an ass farts.
15. If you own two houses, it's raining in one of them.
16. He who bends over too far shows his rear end.
17. Nothing ventured, nothing gained.
18. If something isn't handsome by nature, it's useless for them to wash over and over again.
19. He who has nothing will not eat, if you want flour, you gather chestnut.
20. He who does not know how to plant will plant in November.
21. He who lives fast goes straight to his death.
22. A company drags a man to scaffold.
23. The woman makes the man.
24. Hunger drives the wolf from its den.
25. Pulled too far, a rope ends up in breaking.
26. Through falls and stumbles, one learns to walk.

27. The word goes out but the message is lost.
28. A curse turns against the one who uttered it.
29. A curse turns around and strikes the one who uttered it in the face.
30. A thin cat and fat a woman are the shame of a household.
31. At the end of many disasters, there's always an Italian.
32. Words have no bones but can break bones.
33. By firelight an old rag looks like sturdy hemp fabric.
34. Theory dominates practice.
35. The most beautiful laughter comes from the mouth of a mourner.
36. As there is Easter, so there are meager times.
37. Even the king saves money.
38. Through bumps, one learns to walk.
39. An open path never seems long.
40. Have respect at table and in bed.
41. A good dog gets a good bone.
42. Little by little measure is filled.
43. The vine says to the vintager "make me poor and I will make you rich".
44. Life is just as long as the time it takes for someone to pass by a window.
45. The fox can lose his fur but not his cunning.
46. Next to the fire, straw isn't good.
47. If a caged bird isn't singing for love, it's singing in rage.
48. Have faith and God will provide.
49. Heaven help those who help themselves.
50. Flatter the mother to get the girl.

51. Love and lords want only to be alone together.
52. Even honours are punishment.
53. She flies into rage over a penny.
54. Blood is thicker than water.
55. Water in July is good for nothing.
56. A fine rain still soaks you to the bone, but no one takes it seriously.
57. The morning rainbow reaches the fountain; the evening rainbow fills the sail.
58. A crazy father and mother make sensible children.
59. Long live headdress because hats come and go.
60. Home among home and grapevine among grapevine.
61. Once horse is old, ticks and flies flock to it.
62. He, who lives on hope, dies on shit.
63. What can a cat do if its master is crazy?
64. He who seeks finds.
65. Nothing is blacker than the pan.
66. He who injures with sword will be finished by the sword.
67. Those who are born of chicken scratch the earth.
68. He who kills with a bullet will die by a bullet.
69. One who scorns is the one who buys.
70. He who changes suffers.
71. You have to come into the world in order to enjoy the world.
72. An idle man is up to no good.
73. Those who sleep with children wake up with shit on their asses.
74. He, who has money and friends, turn his nose at justice.

75. He, who does not grow old, is deprived of life.
76. He, who leaves and returns, had a good trip.
77. He, who goes slowly, goes surely and he who goes surely goes far.
78. He, who wins the first hand, leaves with only his pants in hand.
79. To make your neighbour jealous, go to bed early and wake up early.
80. He, who wants to have arms and necessities, can take them himself.
81. Leave the spool to the artisan.
82. Let not your left hand see what your right hand does (Bible Matt: 6v3).
83. That which is written in heaven, comes to pass on earth.
84. Every source flows to the sea.

Cuban

1. A lie runs until it is overtaken by the truth.
2. A lie runs until truth catches up to it.
3. A love that can last forever takes but a second to come about.
4. A man possesses beauty in his quality and a woman possesses quality in her beauty.
5. Brief encounter can result in long relationship.
6. Cheese, wine and a friend must be old to be good.
7. Coffee from the top of the cup and chocolate from the bottom.
8. Do not excessively timid or excessively confident.
9. Do not run into debt with a rich man, or promise anything to poor one.
10. Even a leaf does not flatter on the tree without the will of God.
11. Every head is a world.
12. Faces of men we see but not their hearts.
13. Gluttony and vanity grow with age.
14. God made us and we wonder at it.
15. He who owes nothing has bought nothing on layaway.
16. He, who speaks much, errs much.
17. He who tells the truth doesn't sin, but he calls many inconveniences.
18. How can you trust anyone who doesn't know how to blush?
19. If you return an ass' kick, most of the pain is yours.
20. If you would like to be respected, seek the society of your equals and not of your superiors.

21. Jovial companionships make this dull life tolerable.
22. Justice is a good thing, only not in my house, but in my neighbour's.
23. Kittens are a child's instrument for happiness.
24. Life is short, but it barely takes a second to smile.
25. Listen to what they say about others and you will know what they say of you.
26. Listening looks easy, but it's not that simple, every head is a world.
27. One washes the body in vain, if one does not wash the soul.
28. Seven sons of the mother, and each one of a different mind.
29. Tell me what company you keep and I will tell you who you are.
30. The best of hunters lies more than he hunts.
31. The wise man never says, I did not think.
32. There does never want an excuse for drinking.
33. There is no better mirror than the face of an old friend.
34. There is no agreement under pressure.
35. There is no evil that last a hundred years, nor a body that can endure it.
36. When the monkey talks, everyone else is silent.
37. When the sun rises, it rises for everyone.
38. You cannot distinguish between a drunken and a mad man until they have slept.

Democratic Republic of Congo (Zaire)

1. A small axe is not sufficient to cut down a large tree.
2. Even without drumbeats bananas leaves dance.
3. The sun shines during the day, not at night.
4. The hand assists the foot, but the foot cannot do the same.
5. Clothes should not be made for unborn child.
6. You are invited to join the hunt when your nests are in evidence.
7. A knife does not recognize its owner.
8. The new moon cannot come until the other has gone.
9. Every dog knows the home of your home.
10. A stolen object does not fill one heart with joy.
11. The toad that wanted to avoid the rain fell in water.

Denmark

1. Better to ask twice than to lose your way once.
2. A lazy boy and warm bed difficult to part.
3. He who builds according to every man's advice will have a crooked house.
4. Give to a pig when it grunts and a child when it cries and you will have a fine pig and a bad child.
5. A single bag of money is stronger than two bags of truth.
6. A good example is like a bell that calls many to church.
7. Ask advice only of your equals.
8. Bad is never good until worse happens.
9. He is most cheated who cheats himself.
10. He who is afraid to ask is ashamed of learning.
11. He who would leap high must take a long run.
12. He who takes the child by the hand takes the mother by the heart.
13. It is better to suffer for the truth than to prosper by falsehood.
14. A bad tree does not try to yield good apples.
15. The greater the fear the nearer the danger.
16. God gives all birds their food but does not drop it into their nests.
17. Shared sorrow is half sorrow.
18. Relatives are the worst friends, said the fox as the dogs took after him.
19. Don't say out further than you can grow back.
20. Act honestly and answer boldly.
21. Blind hen also finds grains.
22. Don't brush your teeth before you have opened your mouth.

23. The one who loves you punish.
24. He who takes no chances wins nothing.
25. Where there is no action, there is no waste.
26. No roses without thorns.
27. Many small brooks make the river strong
28. If you save a little here and a little there, you eventually get rich.
29. Necessity teaches the naked woman to spin (a yarn).
30. Don't skin the bear before shooting the bear.
31. It is the thief who thinks that all men steal.
32. Work makes the mater.
33. Keep me signed on this computer unless sign out.
34. A good neighbour is better than a brother far off.
35. Break one link and the whole chain falls apart.
36. It will come back "said the man, when he gave his sow pork".
37. A slip of the foot may soon be recovered, but that of the tongue perhaps never.
38. Age may wrinkle the face, but lack of enthusiasm wrinkles the soul.
39. Faults are thick where love is thin.
40. A crowd is not a company.
41. A fool only wins the first the game.
42. Keep your nose out of another's mess.
43. A friend's frown is better than a fool's smile.
44. Better a little furniture than empty house.
45. It easy to manage when fortunes favours.
46. A bold attempt is half success.
47. He that does not save pennies will never have pounds.
48. A penny in time is as good as a dollar.

49. Kind words don't wear out the tongue.
50. A bird may be ever so small, it always seek a nest of its own.
51. Let deeds match words.
52. Speaking silence is better than senseless speech.
53. A good pilot is not known when the sea is calm and weather fair.
54. He that enquires much learns much.
55. A short rest is always good.
56. That which must be will be.
57. A willing helper does not wait until he is asked.
58. You may always find an opportunity in your sleeves, if you like.
59. Life begins at forty.
60. A man's character reaches town before his person.
61. Another man's burden is always light.
62. Better a little in peace and with right, than much with anxiety and strife.
63. A bold man has luck in his train.
64. Blame is the lazy man's wages.
65. It is easy to sit at the helm in fine weather.
66. A child must creep until it learns to walk.
67. Speedy execution is the mother of good fortune.
68. Advice after injury is like medicine after death.
69. Where you cannot climb over, you must creep under.
70. A good plan today is better than a perfect plan tomorrow.
71. Stop and smell the roses.
72. A little stone may upset a large cart.
73. Better half a loaf than none at all.

74. You can have too much of a good thing.
75. Even a small star shines in darkness.
76. The road to a friend's house is never long.
77. Nothing prolong open sin a much as the postponement of due vengeance.
78. People who grasp at someone else's goods are frequently stripped of their own.
79. It need a powerful bird to wrest they prey from another's claws.
80. Squabbling pigs often from solid front when threatened by wolves.
81. Eagle tears at one another with beak and talons.
82. It is better for a slave to perish than his lord.
83. Your retainer should serve you as tongs do a blacksmith.
84. That's how the stern becomes the prow when the sea grows rough.

Dutch

1. The sun rises for free.
2. When the moon is full, it shines everywhere.
3. His moon is already breaking the clouds.
4. After the rain, the sun will shine.
5. Who needs the moon when the sun is shining?
6. If the sky comes down, not a pole will be left upright.
7. It is raining pipe-stem.
8. If all fools could fly, the sun would be eclipsed forever.
9. Red morning sky brings water to the ditch.
10. High tree catch a lot of wind.
11. As the wind blows, so does his jacket.
12. He, who has butter on his head, should stay out of the sun.
13. He cannot see the sun shines in the water.
14. Unable to see the forest because of the trees.
15. The best steersmen are ashore.
16. It ain't the worst fruit that is eaten by wasps.
17. That breaks my wooden shoe.
18. If it rains in September, x-mas will be in December.
19. The first hit is worth a dollar.
20. There water isn't worth the cabbage.
21. He, who is born for a dime, will never be worth a quarter.
22. Tasty is just one finger long.
23. The future is a book with seven locks.
24. What is the use of candle and glasses if the owls don't want to see?
25. Later-street leads directly to the Never-house.

26. If you don't have a horse, use a donkey.
27. What the peasant does not know, he doesn't eat.
28. A fool can ask more than a hundred, wise men can answer.
29. The devil always shit on the biggest pile.
30. Bitter is the mouth makes the heart healthy.
31. To throw away the child with the bath water
32. What fills the heart will flow over from the mouth.
33. Sunset is useless; the sun has to rise again in the morning anyway.
34. A sewing machine sews but a staple staples.
35. I won't say my prayer for 'brown beans'.
36. Wealth is a temporary thing; it waxes and wanes like the moon.
37. A ring around the moon is not too bad, but a ring around the sun makes a woman and children sad.
38. When the moon is a boat, no rain will fall.
39. When the sun shines on the New Year's Day, it will be a good apple year.
40. No one can make a fabric so fine that it won't be exposed to the sun.
41. Backing the winds and pleasure – seeking women are not to be trusted.
42. Even rain of pigs doesn't give you a brush.
43. If it rains on the Great, it drips on the little people.
44. He, who spits at heaven, spits in his own face.
45. Without mine and theirs, the world would be like heaven.
46. If the sky is all blue, it soon will turn to gray again.

47. The windmill doesn't care for the wind that is gone past.
48. Where the dyke is lowest, water runs over it first.
49. "Every little bit helps", the mosquito said, just before it pissed into the sea.
50. The more people drown in a wineglass then in the sea.
51. If booze is in the man, wisdom is in the can.
52. He, who is in a hurry, shouldn't ride a donkey.
53. A beard were a sign of wisdom, the he-goat would be the wisest.
54. A bearded man is a woman provided for.
55. He, who doesn't find himself important, isn't doing his job well.
56. I don't like children, being one was bad enough.
57. You cannot build a railroad without crossfire.
58. Delicious dreams, brave little dog.
59. Some people eat biscuits in order to save on bread.
60. He is such a liar! you can feel it with your wooden shoes.
61. It is not difficult to become a farmer, but it is difficult to remain a farmer.
62. They are fishing behind the net.
63. He has a house with silver tiles.
64. What does a dog understand about rats and mice?
65. Who serves two masters has to lie to one.
66. The strength of a tree lies in the roots —not is branches.
67. If wealth were divided today according to reason a lot of rich people would be poor tomorrow.

68. Where there are people, there are customers.
69. His pants are always fastening on the second clasp.
70. If it were a dog, it would have bitten you already.
71. It is better that the bakers are on horseback than the doctors.
72. He is sniffing the ground like a dog on the potato field from the farmers.
73. Even if it rained milk, his bowl would be upside down.
74. If you are not doing the cooking, you can't give away the spoon.
75. He is sticking his hand in a wasp nest.
76. He wants to learn how to shave using my beard.
77. A kiss without a beard is like an egg without salt.
78. He talks like a sausage with fat.
79. Whoever wants to sit on two chairs at the same time, will hit the ground.
80. When old dogs bark, it's time to watch out.
81. He is eating with long teeth.
82. He's got it as busy as the hens before Easter.
83. He fell with his nose in the butter.
84. He is putting too much hay on his pitchfork.
85. He's forgotten his worn shoes.
86. You never know how a cow catches a rabbit.
87. You've got to stare the cat down out of the tree.
88. I wish that he would sink as deep in the ground as a hare can run in ten years.
89. It's easy to cut a big chunk from someone else's cheese.
90. When butter gets expensive, you learn to eat your bread dry.

91. It is better to ride for half a year on a good horse than to spend your entire life riding on a mule.
92. A beggar's estate lies in all lands.
93. A blind man may sometimes shoot a crow.
94. A cat that meweth much catches but few mice.
95. A cock is valiant on his own dunghill.
96. A cow-year, a sad year, a bull year, a glad year.
97. A daily guest is a great thief in the kitchen.
98. A dog with a bone knows no friend.
99. A flying crow always catches something.
100. A fool and his money are soon parted.
101. A fool may give a wise man counsel.
102. A fool may chance to say a wise thing.
103. A fool may meet with good fortune, but the wise only profit by it.
104. A friend at one's back is a safe bridge.
105. A friend is better than money in a purse.
106. A friend's dinner is soon dressed.
107. A good fire makes a quick cook.
108. A good friend is better than silver and gold.
109. A good horse is worth his fodder.
110. A good name is better than oil.
111. A great book is a great evil.
112. A guest like fish, stinks the third day.
113. A guilty conscience needs no accuser.
114. A handful of patience is worth more than a bushel of brains.
115. A handful of trade, a handful of gold.
116. A horse may stumble, though he has four legs.
117. A horse full of daughters is a cellar full of sour beer.

118. A hundred baker, a hundred millers and a hundred tailors are three hundred thieves.
119. A hundred man can make an encampment, but it requires a woman to make home.
120. A little spoon is soon hot.
121. A man is known till he cometh to honour.
122. A man must eat, though every tree were a gallows.
123. A man overboard, a mouth the less.
124. A man without money is like a ship without sails.
125. A merry host makes merry guests.
126. A penny spared is better than a florin gained.
127. A penny worth of myrrh is worth a pound of sorrow.
128. A plaster house, a horse at grass, a friend in words, is all mere glass.
129. A plough that worketh shines but still water stinks.
130. A runaway monk never speak well of his convent.
131. A sad bride makes a glad wife.
132. A scabby head fears the comb.
133. A ship on the beach is a light house to the sea.
134. Even if a monkey wears a gold ring, it is and remains an ugly creature.
135. You learn by practice.
136. If you must, you can do a lot.
137. When two dogs fight over a bone, a third one carried it away.
138. Better a good neighbour than a distant friend.
139. The best helmsmen stand on the shore.
140. One person's death is another's bread.
141. The last pieces of lead are heaviest.

142. The sunrise hour has gold in its mouth.
143. The road to hell is paved with good intentions.
144. Desire the father of thought.
145. Think before acting and whilst acting still thinks.
146. A cheeky person owns half the world.
147. A donkey does not bump into the same stone twice.
148. A good start is half the job done.
149. An understanding person needs only half a word.
150. Half an egg is better than empty shell.
151. One swallow doesn't make summer.
152. He is a brick short of a full load (lose screw).
153. Do not wake sleeping dogs.
154. Hasty speed is rarely good.
155. The blood creeps where it can't go.
156. When being too greedy one should expect to be punished.
157. The purpose sanctions the means.
158. If you want something, everything is allowed.
159. Life is not always about roses.
160. Shared grief is half grief.
161. A done deal cannot be reserved.
162. He feels like a cat in a strange warehouse.
163. The louder the person shouts, the less he knows.
164. Hopes sustain life.
165. High tree catches a lot of wind.
166. In the land of the blind, one eye is king.
167. Every advantage has disadvantage.

Egyptian

1. One foot isn't enough to walk with.
2. Our senses serve to affirm not to know.
3. We mustn't confuse Mastery with Mimicry, knowledge with superstitious ignorance.
4. Physical consciousness is indispensable for the achievements of knowledge.
5. A man can't be judged by his neighbour's intelligence; his own vital experience is never his neighbours.
6. No discussion can throw light if it wonders from the real point.
7. Your body is the temple of knowledge.
8. Experience will show you, a master can only point the way.
9. A house has the character of the man who lives in it.
10. All organs work together in the functioning of the whole.
11. A pupil may show you by his own effort how much he deserves to learn from you.
12. Routine and prejudice distort vision. Each man thinks his own horizon is the limit of the word.
13. You will free when you learn to be neutral and follow the instructions of your heart without letting things perturb you. This is the way of Maat.
14. Growth in consciousness doesn't depend on the will of the intellect or it's possibilities but on the intensity of the inner urge.
15. Judge by cause, not effect.

16. Every man must act in the rhythm of the time...such wisdom.
17. Men need images lacking them they invent idols. Better then to find images on realities that lead to the true seeker, to the source.
18. Have the wisdom to abandon the values of a time that has passed and pick up constituent of the future. An environment must be suited to the age and men to their environment.
19. Always watch and follow nature.
20. All seeds answer light, but the colour is different.
21. The plant reveals what is in the seed.
22. Popular belief on essential matters must be examined in order to discover the original thought.
23. It is the passive resistance from the helm that steers the boat.
24. The key to all problems is the problem of consciousness.
25. If you would build something solid, don't works with the wind, always look for a fixed point, something you know that is stable yourself.
26. If you would know yourself, take yourself as a starting point and go back to its source, your beginning will disclose your end.
27. Images are nearer reality than cold definitions.
28. Seek peacefully, you will find.
29. Organization is impossible unless those who know the laws of harmony lay the foundation.
30. It is no use whatever preaching wisdom to men; you must inject it into their blood.

31. Knowledge is consciousness of reality; reality is the sum of the law that govern nature and of the causes from which they flow.
32. Social good is what brings peace to family and society.
33. Knowledge is not necessarily wisdom.
34. By knowing one reaches belief, by doing gains conviction when you dare know, dare.
35. Altruism is the mark of superior being.
36. All is within yourself, know your most inward self and look for what correspond with its nature.
37. The seed cannot sprout upward without simultaneously sending roots into the ground.
38. Grain must return to the earth, die and decompose for new growth to begin.
39. The first concerning the secret, all cognition comes from inside, we are therefore initiated only by ourselves, but the master gives the key.
    - The second concerning the way; the seeker has need of a master to guide him and lift him up when he fall, to lead him back to the right way when he strays.
40. Understanding develops by degrees.
41. As to deserving, know that the gift of Heaven is free, this gift of knowledge is so great that no effort whatever could hope to deserve it.
42. If the master teaches what is error, the disciples' submission is slavery, if he teaches truth, this submission is ennoblement.
43. The only thing that is humiliation is helplessness.

44. An answer is profitable in proportion to the intensity of the quest.
45. Listen to your conviction, even if they seem absurd to your reason.
46. Know the world in yourself; never look for yourself in the world for this would be to project your illusions (to teach one must know the nature of those whom one is teaching).
47. In every vital activity it is the path that matter.
48. The way of knowledge is narrow.
49. Each truth you learn will be for you, as new as if it had never been written.
50. The only active force that arises out of possession is fear of losing object of possession.
51. If you defy an enemy by doubting his courage you doubt it.
52. The nut doesn't reveal the tree it contains.
53. For knowledge...you should know that peace is an indispensable condition of getting it.
54. The first thing necessary in teaching is a master; the second is a pupil capable of carrying the tradition.
55. Peace is the fruit of activity, not of sleep.
56. Envious greed must govern to posses and ambition must possess to govern.
57. When the governing class isn't chosen for quality it is chosen for material wealth, this always means decadence, the lowest stage a society can reach.
58. The best and the shortest road towards knowledge of truth is nature.
59. For every joy there is a practice to be paid.

60. If his heart rules him, his conscience will soon take the place of the rod.
61. What you are doing does not matter so much as what you are learning from doing it.
62. If you search for the laws of harmony, you will find knowledge.
63. If you are searching for a Neter, observe nature.
64. The body is the house of God.
65. True teaching is not the accumulation of knowledge; it is an awakening of consciousness which goes through successive stages.
66. The man who knows how to lead one of his brothers towards what he has known may one day be saved by the very brother.
67. People bring about their own undoing through their tongue.
68. If one tries to navigate unknown waters one runs the risk of shipwreck.
69. Leave him to error who loves his error.
70. Every man is rich in excuses to safeguard his prejudice, his instinct and his opinions.
71. To know means to record in one's memory but to understand means to blend with the things and assimilate it oneself.
72. There are two kinds of errors; blind credulity and piecemeal criticism, never believe a word without putting its truth to test.
73. Love is one thing, knowledge is another.
74. True sages are those who give what they have without meanness and without secret.

75. An answer brings no illumination unless the question has matured to a point where it gives rise to this which thus becomes its fruit.

76. Whatever reveals itself to me ceases to be mysterious, for me alone, if I unveil it to anyone else, he hears mere words which betrays the living sense, profanation, but never revelation.

77. May know thyself and thou shall know the gods.

78. The seed includes all possibilities of the bee...the seed will develop these possibilities, however only if it receives corresponding energies from the sky.

79. A beautiful thing is never perfect.

80. A man's ruin lies in his tongue.

81. Be patient with a bad neighbour; he may move or face misfortune.

82. Because we focus on the snake, we missed the scorpion.

83. Bed is the poor man's opera.

84. False ambition serves the neck.

85. If there were no faults, there would be no pardon.

86. Learn politeness from impolite.

87. Making money selling manure is better than losing money selling musk.

88. Malice drinketh its own poison.

89. Pride and dignity would belong to women if only men would leave them alone.

90. Pride feels no pain.

91. Pride goes before a fall.

92. Pride goes before destruction and a haughty spirit before fall.

93. Put a rope around your neck and many will be to drag you along.
94. Put a stout heart to a steep hill.
95. Put a stout heart to stay brave.
96. Put by for a rainy day.
97. Run as hard as a wild beast if you will, but you won't get any reward greater than that destined for you.
98. The barking of a dog does not disturb the man on a camel.
99. The tyrant is the only slave turned inside out.
100. When the angels present themselves, the devil absconds.
101. It is better not to know and to know that one does not know, than presumptuously to attribute some random meaning to symbols.
102. Exuberance is a good stimulus towards action, but the inner light grows in silence and concentration.
103. Not the greatest master can go even one step for his discipline; in himself he must experience each stage of developing consciousness. Therefore he will know nothing for which he is not right.

English

1. Every path has its puddle.
2. The eyes are the window of the soul.
3. A full cup must be carried steadily.
4. Don't fall before you are pushed.
5. Use soft words and hard arguments.
6. A man is old as he feels himself to be.
7. A smooth sea never made a skilled mariner.
8. A stumble may prevent fall.
9. Absence sharpness love, presence strengthens it.
10. Danger and delight grow on stalk.
11. Give neither advice nor salt, until you are asked for it.
12. He that plant trees loves others besides himself.
13. The best are always in the wrong.
14. Write down the advice of him who loves you though you like it not at present.
15. A good chief gives, he does not take.
16. Remember that your children are not your own, but are lent to you by the creator.
17. Regard Heaven as your father, Earth as your mother and all things as your brothers and sisters.
18. The soul would have no rainbow if the eye had no tears.
19. Coyote is always out there waiting and coyote is always hungry.
20. There is nothing as eloquent as a rattle snake tail.
21. A rocky vineyard does not need a prayer, but a pick tax.
22. Every animal knows more than you do.
23. White men have many chiefs.

24. To touch the earth is to have harmony with the nature.
25. When a fox walks lame, the old rabbit jumps.
26. A starving man will eat with the wolf.
27. The coward shoots with shut eyes.
28. It is easy to be brave from a distance.
29. A bird that has eaten cannot fly with the bird that is hungry.
30. Do not wrong or hate your neighbour for it is not he that you wrong but yourself.
31. Make my enemy brave and strong, so that if defeated, I will not be ashamed.
32. Cherish youth, but trust old age.
33. Sharing and giving are the ways of God.
34. We are all one child spinning through mother sky.
35. Each person is his own judge.
36. Sing your death song and die like a hero going home.
37. We are made from mother earth and we go back to mother earth.
38. It is no longer good enough to cry peace; we must act peace, live peace and live in peace.
39. A danger foreseen is half avoided.
40. Our first teacher is our heart.
41. All who have died are equal.
42. One rain does not make a crop.
43. Man's law changes with his understanding of man only the law of the spirit remain always the same.
44. Old age is no honourable as death, but most people want it.
45. You already possess everything necessary to become great.

46. We will be known forever by the tracks we leave.
47. There is no death, only the change of worlds.
48. Day and night cannot dwell together.
49. In age, talk, in childhood tears.
50. One finger cannot lift a pebble.
51. All dreams spinout from the same web.
52. The one who tells the stories rules the world.
53. The rain falls on the just and unjust.
54. Don't be afraid to cry, it will free your mind of sorrowful thoughts.
55. Wisdom comes only when you stop looking for it and start living the life the creator intended for you.
56. A rainbow is a sign from Him who is in all things.
57. A brave man dies but once, a coward many times.
58. Walk lightly in the spring mother earth is pregnant.
59. When a man moves away from nature his heart becomes hard.
60. Force no matter how concealed, begets resistance.
61. Everything the power does, it does in circle.
62. A man or a woman with many children has many homes.
63. Seek wisdom, not knowledge. Knowledge is of the past, wisdom is of the future.
64. Everyone who is successful must have dreamed of something.
65. If you see no reason of giving thanks, the fault lies in yourself.
66. Hope is the nurse of misery.

67. If you don't have a plan for yourself, you will be part of someone else's.
68. If you look back, you will soon be going that way.
69. If you take care of your character, your reputation will take care of itself.
70. It is less of a problem to be poor, than to be dishonest.
71. It is better to have less thunder in the mouth and more lighting in the hand.
72. Each bird loves to hear itself sing.
73. All plants are our brothers and sisters, they talk to us and if we listen, we can hear them.
74. Take only what you need and leave the lands as you found it.
75. Before eating, always take time to thank the food.
76. When we show respect for other living things, they respond with respect for you.
77. If you wonder often, the gift of knowledge will come.
78. Most of us do not look as handsome to others as we do to others.
79. Those that lie down with dog get up with fleas.
80. Life is not separate from death, it only looks that way.
81. What is life? It is the flesh of a firefly in the night. It is the breath of a buffalo in the winter time. It is the little shadows which across the grass and looses itself in the sunset.
82. When you were born, you cried and the world rejoiced. Live your life so that when you die, the world cries and you rejoiced.

83. Don't let yesterday use up too much of today.
84. If a man is as wise as a serpent, he can afford to be as harmless as a dove.
85. The weakness of the enemy makes our strength.
86. A soldier is a poor scout.
87. Beware of the man who does not talk, and the dog that does no bark.
88. Do not judge your neighbour until you walk two moons in his moccasins.
89. With all things and in all things, we are relative.
90. Poverty is a noose, that strangle humanity and breeds disrespect for God and man.
91. The frog does not drink up the pond in which he lives.
92. The moon is not ashamed by the barking of dogs.
93. Listening to a liar is like drinking warm water.
94. Listen or your tongue will keep you deaf.
95. If a man is to do something more than human, he must have more than human.
96. Even a small mouse has anger.
97. Not every sweet root gives birth to sweet grass.
98. Those who have one foot in the canoe, and one foot in the boat, are going to fall into river.
99. They are not dead who live in the heart they leave behind.
100. The way of a trouble maker is thorny.
101. God gives us each a song.
102. When you die, you will be spoken of as those in the sky like the stars.
103. Take only memories leave nothing but footprint.

104. When the earth is sick, the animal will begin to disappear when that happens the warrior of the Rainbow will come to save them.
105. All things are connected, whatever befalls the earth; befall the sons of the Earth. Man did not weave the web of life. He is merely a strand in it. Whatever he does to the web, he does to himself.
106. So live your life that the fear of death can never enter your heart. Trouble no one their religion, respect others in their view and demand that they respect yours.

Ethiopian

1. When the spider web unites, they tie up a lion.
2. Grow old is mandatory, growing up is optional.
3. He who conceal his disease, cannot be cure.
4. Women should remain at home, sit still, keep house and bear and bring up children.
5. Shake at your feet and stick at your hand.
6. The witness of a rat is another rat.
7. He who learns teaches.
8. Woman without a man is like a field without a seed.
9. Unless you call out, who will open the door?
10. When the heart overflows, it comes out through the mouth.
11. You cannot build a house for the last year's summer.
12. The fool speaks, the wise man listens.
13. A cat may go to monastery but she still remains a cat.
14. A silly daughter teaches her mother how to bear children.
15. It is easy to become a monk in one's old age.
16. The fool is thirsty in the midst of water.
17. One's name remains above the grave.
18. As the wound inflames the tiger, so thought inflames the mind.
19. Move your neck according to the music.

Faroese Islands

1. When ale goes in the wit goes out.
2. After a landslide one more can be expressed.
3. An eager dog often gets a torn skin.
4. As we egged on, we rage.
5. Better be a good man's slave than badly married.
6. Better leave something than eating overly much.
7. Better own it than asking your brother for it.
8. Big rivers are made out of small brooks.
9. Blind is the bookless man.
10. Burnt child fears fire.
11. Done by oneself is well done.
12. Everything is better than owing nothing.
13. Haste often causes hasty things.
14. He that rows out often gets fish at last.
15. He who waits get tail wind and he who rows a harbor.
16. Heavy is an old man's fall.
17. High calling brings high fall.
18. If a dane first comes into the room, more danes will probably follow.
19. It is a poor mouse that doesn't have more than one hole.
20. It is best to ask a man who manages on his own.
21. It is better to attract two birds to the nest than one.
22. It is good to wait for a man that is alive.
23. It mars to tie the dog to the butter stump.
24. It's a poor bird that fouls its own nest.
25. It's better to have to trust in others.
26. It is better to be prepared than swift afterwards.

27. It's difficult to build a boat plant against the wave.
28. It's the owner of the two cows who walks close to her tail.
29. Keep silence won't get you court.
30. Wool is the gold of the Faroes (Faroes Island).
31. Loans are to come home (back) laughing.
32. Many can carry things on both shoulders.
33. No one should forget old friends and old goats.
34. Nobody is to eat the morsel of someone else.
35. None reaches further than his arm reach.
36. Nothing is bad that isn't good for nothing.
37. Nothing ventured, nothing won.
38. Old ones are good at counselling.
39. Old ravens are not easy to fool.
40. See the guest out if you want to see him again.
41. Small birds lay small eggs.
42. Small boat sail, as well as ship.
43. Small fish are better than empty dishes.
44. Swimming is easy if someone holds your head above the water.
45. The blind one asked the naked guy to lead him on.
46. The child does not cry as long as it has its way.
47. The coward falls.
48. The crow thinks best of her own chickens.
49. The dead man's heir are many, but not his brothers.
50. The dog is as his master (like master, like dog).
51. The food we grow ourselves is fit.
52. The knifeless man is a lifeless man.
53. The one who derides others get derides too.

54. The thief believes that everybody steals.
55. There are misfortunes in almost every family.
56. There is always something the matter with a bad child.
57. There lies often falsehood beneath a pretty skin.
58. There should be good ember after a good life.
59. Things don't always go as planned.
60. Time runs like a river current.
61. We are born to be our own and not fed to it.
62. When the mouse is satisfied the flour is bitter.
63. Who does not eat till he is full won't lick himself satisfied.
64. Who fares suitably (carefully) get ahead.
65. Who is reared at home fares wrong away from home.
66. Who rides first, controls the speed.
67. You can take an ox to the river, but begging it won't make it drink.
68. You have made your bed, so you can like in it.

French

1. Nothing is impossible for a willing heart.
2. To a Valliant heat nothing is impossible.
3. No one is bound to do the impossible.
4. Unhappiness is good for nothing.
5. The tree often hides the forest.
6. Desperate times call for desperate measures.
7. To the great evils great medicines.
8. With ifs and butts, one would put Paris in a bottle.
9. Immediately said, immediately done.
10. Goods poorly have gotten never profit.
11. Immediately said immediately done.
12. A good name is better than riches.
13. Well named is worth than golden belt.
14. What's bred in the bone will come out in the flesh.
15. Good blood does not know how to lie.
16. You have made your bed, now you must lie on it.
17. There will be bumps on the smoothest roads.
18. Between the tree and the bark one should not put a finger.
19. Punctuality is the politeness of kings.
20. No pain no gain.
21. You need break the shell to have the almond.
22. Never say never.
23. Never say die.
24. One should never throw the handle after the felling axe.
25. Leaving nothing to chance.
26. There are none so distant that fate cannot bring together.

27. It is better to be a hammer than a nail / anvil.
28. There is no such word as "cant" impossible isn't French.
29. There is no telling what tomorrow will bring.
30. Better to bend than to break.
31. Better late than never.
32. Walls have ears.
33. A warm Christian means a cold Easter.
34. You can't make omelets without breaking the eggs.
35. You can't have your cake and eat it too.
36. You can't have butter and the money from the butter.
37. You can't be in two places at once.
38. One only lends to be rich.
39. Tall oaks from little acorns grow.
40. The little streams make big rivers.
41. He who loves well punishes well.
42. He who breaks the glasses pays for them.
43. He who fears dangers shouldn't go to the sea.
44. If you can't stand the heat, get out of the kitchen.
45. Charity will be rewarded in heaven.
46. He who gives the poor loans God.
47. He who sleeps forgets hunger.
48. Once the first step is taken up there's no going back.
49. When wine is drawn, one must drink it.
50. He who loves me loves my dog.
51. Hear the other side and believe little.
52. He who hears only one bell hears only sound.
53. He who risks nothing has nothing.
54. He who can do more can do less.

55. He who marries in haste repents in leisure.
56. He who saws the wind reaps the storm.
57. If the shoes fits, wear it.
58. He who feels stuffy should blow his nose.
59. He who has land has quarrels.
60. He who grasps too much loses everything.
61. He who hugs too much hold badly.
62. He, who leaves his place, loses it.
63. He who goes hunting loses his place.
64. He who goes slowly goes merely.
65. The end justifies the means.
66. He who takes it slow and steady travels a long way.
67. He who wants to travel far spares his mount.
68. What will be will be.
69. He who lives will see.
70. The strongest reason is always the best.
71. Slow and steady wins the race.
72. Whoever laughs last laugh best.
73. Youth is wasted on the young.
74. Laugh on Friday, cry on Sunday.
75. All tastes are in nature.
76. All's well that ends well.
77. All things come to those who wait.
78. The labour is worthy of his hire.
79. All trouble taken deserves pay.
80. The truth comes out of the mouth of children.
81. To want, that's to be able.
82. Big problem requires big solutions.
83. For larger evils, great remedies.
84. Each one is a craft man of his own fortune.
85. The wolf eases the ewe he is told of.

86. Each one knows where the pack wounds.
87. It is good to have more than one anchor on the ship.
88. In small field good corn grows.
89. Reason lies between the bridle and the spur.
90. Make the wood of a press oar the handle of a cernoir.
91. For lack of the ox, one plough with one donkey.
92. Insane and simple is the ewe that makes the wolf his confessor.
93. One should not judge the tree by the bark.
94. One should not let the grass grow on friendship's road.
95. He has a fine horse that never stumbles.
96. It is better to lose a witty remark than a friend.
97. There are more purchasers than experts.
98. A muffled cat never took mice.
99. The purse opens the mouth.
100. Adversity makes wise.
101. An eagle does not generate the dove, eagles don't breed doves.
102. Love and poverty do bad housework together.
103. The year that is gone is always the best.
104. Money is the nerve of war.
105. Money is round toll.
106. The advice (opinion) of the woman is seldom much priced, but he who does not take it is stupid. A woman's advice is no great thing, but he who won't take it is a fool.
107. The uneven one does not see his bump, but sees that of his fellow-man.
108. The wind never enters the house of lawyer.

109. The old friends and the old ecus are the best.
110. Misery, greedy nature makes a great need of everything.
111. Better an egg in peace than an ox in war.
112. One learns while falling.
113. One does not go to the mill with the beauty of one's wife.
114. Where the wolf finds a lamb there I seek another one.
115. When the tree has fallen everybody runs to the branches.
116. When a fool goes to Rome, there same fool returns from there.
117. Who eats chicken, chicken comes from him.
118. Who does not have money in the purse must have money in the mouth.
119. Who was born a cat pursues the mice.
120. Who makes herself an ewe, the wolf eats her.
121. Receiving without giving turns the friendship.
122. All is well that ends well.
123. A good deed is not without reward.
124. Better buy than borrow.
125. The end of passion is the beginning of repentance.
126. Appearances are deceiving.
127. Who spits against the wind spits in his own face.
128. Who is angry must be pleased again.
129. Stretch your arms no further than your sleeves.
130. Bacchus has drowned more men than Neptune.
131. Fortune helps him that's willing to help himself.
132. The first blow fell not the tree (the first attempt or effort may not amount too much).

133. The cart leads the horse, the young instructs the old.
134. The cart leads the horse, the young instructs the old.
135. Reports make mischief greater than they need to be.
136. He that's asks he would, hear what he would not.
137. One bee makes no swarm.
138. One turn serves another.
139. Don't bark if you can't bite.
140. He that goes borrowing goes sorrowing.
141. A ragged colt may make good horse.
142. A dry cough is the trumpet of death.
143. All is not lost that is delayed.
144. It is very hard to shave an egg.
145. What can't be cured, must be endure.
146. The eye of the master does more than both hands.
147. Who never climbed, never fell.
148. Every flow has its ebb.
149. Save a thief from gallows and he will cut your throat.
150. Tell me with whom you go, and I will tell you what you do.
151. Hope is the dream of a soul awake.

Gambia

1. Making friends / knowing people in high position never hurt.
2. Even the best words, brings no food.
3. Before healing others, heal yourself.
4. The knot tied by a wise man cannot be undone by a fool.
5. Although the snake does not fly, it has caught the hornbill whose home is in the sky.
6. Recognition of valour must be earned.
7. When shield wears out, the framework still remains.
8. Men die, but their words and works live on, or a person's true nature does not change but may only be revealed through adversities.
9. You cannot tell from the quills of a porcupine whether it is prepared to fight or not.
10. One should never bottoms with a porcupine.
11. Don't get into altercation with someone who has more power than you do – such as the chief or you will certainly be the loser.
12. If you are on the road to nowhere, find another road.
13. You must act as if it is impossible to fail.
14. The ruin of a nation begins in the home of its people.
15. Don't follow the path, go where there is no path to begin the trail.
16. Don't let what you cannot tear from your hands what you can.
17. True power comes through cooperation and silence.

18. Two men in a burning house must not stop to argue.
19. One falsehood spoils a thousand truths.
20. If nothing touches the palm – leaves they do not rustle.
21. He is a fool whose sheep runs away twice.

Ghanaian

1. A crab does not beget a bird.
2. A cracked bell can never sound well.
3. Do not call the forest that shelters you a jungle.
4. It is the calm and silent water that drowns a man.
5. It is the fool's sheep that break lose twice.
6. One camel does not make fun of another camel's hump.
7. One falsehood spoils a thousand truths.
8. Two small antelopes can beat a big one.
9. When a man is wealthy he may wear an old cloth.
10. When a man's coat is threadbare, it is easy to pick a whole in it.
11. When the cock is drunk, he forgets about the hawk.
12. The tongue weighs practically nothing, but so few can hold it.
13. The moon moves slowly, but it crosses the town.
14. When a king has good counsellors, his reign is peaceful.
15. When you are rich, you are hated, when you are poor, you are despised.
16. He who is guilty is the one that has much to say.
17. If you understand the beginning well, the end will not trouble you.
18. The poor man and the rich man do not play.
19. Money is sharper than a sword.
20. It is not a shame at all to work for money.
21. If you are hiding, don't light a fire.
22. Even though the old man is strong and heavy, he does live forever.

German

1. A country can be judge by the quality of its proverbs.
2. A hedge between keeps friendship green.
3. A poor person isn't he who has little, but he who needs a lot.
4. As fast as laws are devised, their evasion is contrived.
5. Better an honest enemy than a false friend.
6. Don't praise the day till evening has come.
7. You should study when there is ample time, better study with ample time.
8. Lies are like a snowball, the further they roll, the bigger they get.
9. It is better to raise the dust to get dusty.
10. A bad beginning may make a good ending.
11. A bad cause requires many words.
12. A bad penny always comes back.
13. A baptized Jew is a circumcised Christian.
14. A bashful dog never fattens.
15. A better seldom comes after.
16. A blind horse goes straight forward.
17. A bold does not always fall when it thunders.
18. A bold onset is half the battle.
19. A cat has nine lives, as the onion seven skins.
20. A cat in gloves catches no mice.
21. A cat is a lion to mouse.
22. A clean mouth and honest hand, will take a man through any land.
23. A closed mouth and open eyes never did anyone harm.
24. A blind man swallows many flies.

25. A closed mouth catches no flies.
26. A dainty stomach beggars the purse.
27. A danger foreseen is half avoided.
28. A doctor and a boor know more than a doctor alone.
29. A dam of discretion is worth a pound of wisdom.
30. A drink is shorter than a tale.
31. Dripping June sets all in time.
32. A drop of honey catches more flies than a hogshead of vinegar.
33. A father maintains ten children better than ten children one father.
34. A fence last three years, a dog last three fences, a horse three dogs, and a man three horses.
35. A fence makes love more keen.
36. A fish should swim thrice, in water, in sauce, and in wine.
37. A flatter has water in one hand and fire in the other.
38. A glutton young, a beggar old.
39. A golden hammer breaks an iron gate.
40. A good conscience is a soft pillow.
41. A good meal is worth hanging for.
42. A good name is a rich inheritance.
43. A good speaker makes a good liar.
44. A good trade will carry farther than thousand florins.
45. A gosling flew over the Rhine and came home a goose.
46. A handful of might is better than a sack full of right.

47. A huckster, who cannot pass of mouse – turd of pepper, has not learned his trade.
48. A hug a day keeps the demons at bay.
49. A hundred years of regret pay not a farthing of debt.
50. A hundred years of wrong do not make an hour right.
51. A lawyer and a cart-wheel must be greased.
52. A lean agreement is better than a fat lawsuit.
53. He who borrows sells his freedom.
54. Charity sees the need, not the cause.
55. No answer is also an answer.
56. Luck sometimes visits a fool, but it never sits down with him.
57. To change and to change for the better are two different things.
58. Loquacity and lying are cousins.
59. Rast ich, so rost ich (when I rest, I rust).
60. Buying is cheaper than asking.
61. Revenge converts a little right into a great wrong.

Greek

1. A different man, different taste.
2. A gift though small is welcome.
3. A library is a repository of medicine for the mind.
4. A lucky person is someone who plants pebble and harvest potatoes.
5. A mad bull is not to be tied up with packthread.
6. A miser and a liar bargain quickly.
7. A miser is ever in want.
8. Act quickly, think slowly.
9. After the war, aid.
10. An iron rod bends while it is hot.
11. An open enemy is better than a false friend.
12. Before you can score you must first have a goal.
13. Character is a habit long continued.
14. Death is never at a loss for occasion.
15. Eat and drink with your relative, do business with strangers.
16. Even from a foe a man may learn wisdom.
17. First secure an independent income then practice virtue.
18. From a thorn comes a rose, and from a rose comes a thorn.
19. Good accounts make good friends.
20. Gray hair is a sign of age, not wisdom.
21. Great abilities produce great vice as well as virtues.
22. Great birth is a very poor dish at table.
23. He who cannot bear misfortune is truly unfortunate.
24. He who respects his parents never dies.

25. He who revealeth his secrets maketh himself a slave.
26. I send thee myrrh, not that thou mayest be by it perfumed, but perfumed by thee.
27. If advice will not approve him, neither will the rod.
28. If all men were just, there would be no need of valour.
29. Ignorance of one's misfortune is clear again.
30. Ignorance of the law is no excuse for breaking it.
31. I'll beef never made gude broo.
32. I'll laughter is a dangerous evil.
33. In hospitality, the chief thing is good will.
34. It is easier to talk than hold one's tongue.
35. Keep no secret of thyself from thyself.
36. Kindness begets kindness.
37. Learn to obey before you command.
38. Learn to walk before you run.
39. Live today forget the past.
40. Many pupils have gained more wealth than his master.
41. Many men many minds.
42. Men never moan over opportunities lost to do good only opportunities to be bad.
43. Men prone to tears are good.
44. Many men know how to flatter, few know how to praise.
45. No need to teach an eagle to fly.
46. Observe your enemies, for they first find your faults.
47. Old age and poverty are wounds that can't be healed.

48. Old age and treachery will overcome youth and skill.
49. Old men are twice children.
50. Many words are poverty.
51. A person can be sweet as honey or as a heavy as steel.
52. A society grows when old men plant trees whose shade they know they shall never sit it.
53. As long as you have blessing of your parents it does not matter even if live in the mountains.
54. Either dance well or quit the ballroom.
55. He who is not satisfied with a little is not satisfied with a lot.
56. Help yourself so God can help you.
57. If you are truthful to you will have as much gold as you want.
58. If you do not have brains you follow the same route twice.
59. A small evil may be great.
60. A word out of season may mar a whole lifetime.
61. Add no fire to fire.
62. Affairs sleep soundly when fortune is present.
63. Don't hear one and judge two.
64. Endeavour to bear the ignorance of fortune with patience.
65. He who has been angry becomes cool again.
66. He laughs not in the morning, laughs not at noon.
67. Hunger is the teacher of many.
68. I live too near a wood to be scared by owls.
69. If the sun shines while it rains, the devil is beating his mother.

70. In baiting a mousetrap with cheese, always leave room for the mouse.
71. In hospitality it is the spirits that counts.
72. It is the make who makes the city.
73. Neither promise wax to the saint, nor cake to the child.
74. Nothing will content him who is not content with a little.
75. Poor man's words have little weight.
76. Seize the end and you will hold the middle.
77. The child who gets a stepmother also gets a stepfather.
78. The mills of gods grind slowly, but they grind exceedingly small.
79. The net of a sleeper catches fish.
80. The Sheppard, even when he becomes a gentleman smells of lamb.
81. The silence of a treacherous man is to be feared even more than his words.
82. There's many a slip betwixt the cup and the lip.
83. Thinking evil is much the same as doing it.
84. Those who are thirsty drink in silence.
85. To the brave man every land is a native country.
86. Welcome is the best cheer.
87. With a relation eat and drink, but conduct no business with him.
88. Wood that grows warped can never be straightened.
89. Young hot wood makes hot fire.
90. The liar and the chief rejoice in their first year only.
91. He who suffers much will know much.

92. One minute of patience, ten year of peace.
93. It is not what they profess but what they practice that make them good.
94. If it were not for hope, the heart would break.
95. Those who the gods would destroy, first they would make angry.
96. The heart that loves is always young.
97. A truth spoken before its time is dangerous.
98. When God throws the dice are loaded.
99. Think with the wise, but walk with the vulgar.

Guinea Bissau
1. Milk the cow but do not pull off the udder.
2. The female of the species is more deadly than the male.
3. One of these days is none of these days.
4. If you love him don't lend him.
5. Every peddler praises his own needle.
6. A throne is only a bench covered with velvet.

Gypsy (Romani)

1. He who wants to enslave you will never tell you the truth about your forefathers.
2. Burry me standing, I have been on my knees my whole life.
3. One mad man makes many, madmen, and many madmen makes madness.
4. May you have a lawsuit in which you know you are in the right.
5. A cough will tick longer by a horse than a peck of oats.
6. A dapple-grey horse will sooner dies than tire.
7. A lonely old cow, see someone you know, fly to your right, sure to be right and if you are hawking, money before night.
8. Flies goes to go lean horses.
9. Good horses can't be of a bad colour.
10. He that hath a white horse and a fair wife need never want trouble.
11. In selling a horse praise his bad points and leave the good one to look after themselves.
12. One man may better steal a horse than another look on.
13. The buyer needs a hundred eyes, the horse thief not one.
14. Water trotted is as good as oats.
15. Everyone is the age of his heart.
16. Every old woman is a witch and every old man a wizard.
17. Where should a witch go if not to her kin?
18. Every witch belongs to the devil's gang.

Haitian

1. A borrowed drum never makes good dancing.
2. A little dog is really brave in front of his master's house.
3. An impudent child grows up under baron's eye.
4. Roaches are never right when facing chickens.
5. Remember the rain that made your corn grow.
6. In times of famine, sweet potatoes have no skin.
7. You know how to run, but you don't know how to hide.
8. It is because the toad is too kind-hearted that he has no intelligence.
9. Little by little the bird builds the nest.
10. The constitution is a paper bayonets are steel.
11. A beautiful funeral does no guarantee heaven.
12. A poor malatto is black, a wealthy black is malatto.
13. Just because someone is smiling at you doesn't mean they're your friends.
14. Wife of a time, Mother of all time.
15. An empty sack cannot stand up.
16. Beyond the mountain, more mountains.
17. God acts and doesn't talk.
18. Speaking French doesn't mean you're smart.
19. The donkey sweats so the horse can be decorated with lace.
20. A monkey never thinks her baby is ugly.
21. If work were a good thing the rich would have grabbed it a long time ago.
22. Speak plainly, don't try to deceive.
23. When the Mapou (oak like tree) dies, goats would eat the leaves.

24. A mother never bites her child to the bone.
25. Salt doesn't boast that is salted.
26. If you want to catch a wild horse, find a tight corral.
27. That which does not kill will make you fat.
28. The giver of the blow forgets, the bearer of the scar remembers.
29. The rock in the water does not know the pain of the rock in the sun.
30. If you drink water does not know the pain of the rock in the sun.
31. If it is God who sends you, he will pay your expenses.
32. What you do is what you see.
33. It is the owner of the body who looks out for the body.
34. God says do your part and I will do mine.
35. You know what you have got but you don't know what is coming.
36. Woman is like a mahogany, the older the better.
37. Past years are always better.
38. What happens to the turkey can happen to the roaster too.
39. There is no prayer which does not have an "Amen".
40. After the dance the drum is heavy.
41. Many hands make the load lighter.
42. When they want to kill a dog they say it's crazy.
43. The peoples pencil has no eraser.
44. A leaky house can fool the sun, but can't fool the rain.
45. A protector is like a cloak.

46. A rolling stone gathers no moss.
47. Uproot the manioc, and clear the land.
48. Smelling good is expensive.
49. Hunger is misery, a full stomach is trouble.
50. When you curse your step-mother, your mother will be the victim.
51. A foreseen disaster does not kill the handicapped.
52. The dead do not know when the value of white sheet.
53. The frog's pee adds to the river.
54. Better to take your time on the way, if you bring good news.
55. Little snakes need to grow in hiding.
56. You don't buy a cat in the bag (know what you are buying).
57. You don't throw rocks at a green mango.
58. A stumble is not a fall.
59. Beat the dog, wait for its master.
60. Children aren't dogs, adults aren't gods.
61. Children learn to creep ere they can learn to go.
62. Children have wide ears and long tongues.
63. If someone sweats for you, you change his shirt.
64. If work were good for you, the rich would leave none for the poor.
65. If you do wrong make amends.
66. If you want your eggs hatched, sit on them yourself.
67. Ignorance does not kill you, but it does not make you sweat a lot.
68. Poor people entertain with the heart.
69. The child of tiger is tiger.

70. The child saith nothing but what he heard at the fireside.
71. The crab that walks too far falls into the pot.
72. The goat which has many owners will be left to die in the sun.
73. When the cat's stomach is full, the rat's back is bitter.
74. When the character of a man is not clear to you, look at his friends.
75. I give you a room and now you want my living room.
76. Life is like the ball of a dog, always looking backwards.

Hebrew

1. A little fire burns up a great deal of corn.
2. A rich man has no need of character.
3. Admission by the defendant is worth a hundred witnesses.
4. An advantage of poverty, your relative gains nothing by your death.
5. Do not confine your children to your learning, for they were born in another time.
6. Eat vegetables and fear no creditors rather than eat duck and hide.
7. God did not create a woman from man's head, that he should her, nor from his feet, that he should be his slave, but rather from his side that he should be near his heart.
8. Happy the generation where the great listen to the small, for it follows that in such a generation the small will listen to the great.
9. He who takes his rank lightly raises his own dignity.
10. If a word be worth one shekel, silence is worth two.
11. Love him who tells your faults in private.
12. Make not a fence more expensive or more important than the thing is forced.
13. Make not thy tail broader than thy wings.
14. Opinions founded on prejudice are always sustained with the greatest violence.
15. People worry, and God smiles.
16. Promise little and do much.
17. Rivalry of scholars advances wisdom.
18. Silence is fence around wisdom.

19. Silence is a fine jewel for a woman, but it is little worn.
20. Silence is a woman's best garment.
21. Slander slay three persons, the speaker, the spoken to and the spoken of.
22. Teach thy tongue to say "I do not know".
23. Teach your grandma to spin.
24. Teach your granddame to suck eggs.
25. The court is most merciful when the accused is most rich.
26. The kind man feeds his cat before sitting to dinner.
27. The more you add, the worse it gets.
28. The place honours not the man; it is the man who honours the place.
29. These three are the marks of a Jew – a tender heart, self-respect and charity.
30. Time heals old pain, while it creates new.
31. Time is a great healer.
32. He who seeks more than he needs hinders himself from enjoying what he has.
33. Whoever teaches his son teaches not only his son and so on to the end of generations.
34. You don't show a fool a job half done.
35. Who is the bravest hero? He who turns his enemy into a friend.
36. Pride is the mask we make of our faults.
37. The best way to know a man is to watch him when he is angry.
38. Judge not thy neighbour until thou art come into his place.
39. Commit a sin twice and it will not seem a crime.

40. Do not be wise in words – be wise in deeds.
41. Don't be sweet, lest you eaten up, don't be bitter, lest you spewed out.
42. Don't live in a town where there are no doctors.
43. Don't look for more honour than your learning merits.
44. First mend yourself, and then mend others.

Herero

1. A bitter heart devours its owner.
2. A weak person goes where he is smiled at.
3. You do not run into mountains, but people yes.

Honduran

1. One Indian less, one extra tortilla.
2. The hare jumps when you least expect.
3. Secure ten cents are better than twenty cents in the betting pot.
4. You fart but you never take a dump.
5. Don't suck a mango until it is ripe.
6. Grief shared is half grief, joy shared is double joy.

Iceland

1. Learning has at all times been venerated by Icelanders.
2. A greasy chicken, a will with not much in it.
3. A man yearns for his paradise but it could become his hell.
4. A sitting crow starves.
5. A story is only half told if there is only one side presented.
6. All old sayings have something in them.
7. Bald birds seldom bring good weather.
8. Better to drink milk the milk than to eat the cow.
9. Better wise language than well combed hair.
10. Every man likes the smell of his own farts.
11. Every story has two sides and every song has twelve versions.
12. Everyone wants to live long, but no one wants to be called old.
13. Few are like fathers, no one is like mother.
14. He who lives without disciplines dies without honour.
15. Hunger works and sweat are the best herbs.
16. It is difficult to steal when the boss is a thief.

Indian

1. To watch us dance is to hear our hearts speak.
2. For the friendship of two, the patience of one is required.
3. Life is not a continuum of pleasant choices, but of inevitable problems that call for strength determination and hard work.
4. A smile you sent, it will always return.
5. To the mediocre, mediocrity appears great.
6. Don't judge any man until you walked two moons in his moccasins.
7. I had no shoes and complained until I met a man who had no feet.
8. Where love reign the impossible may be attained.
9. Great anger is more destructive than the sword.
10. Anger is end cruelty.
11. Indian agriculture is best, enterprise is acceptable, but avoid being on the fixes wage.
12. Blaming faults on your nature does not change the nature of your faults.
13. Blow the wind never so fast, it will lower at last.
14. Call on God, but row away from the rocks.
15. Don't bargain for fish which are still in the water.
16. Don't just cross a river – cross it bearing fire.
17. Fate and self help share equally in shaping our destiny.
18. Garlic is as good as ten mothers.
19. Keep five yards from a carriage, ten yards from a horse and hundred yards from an elephant, but the distance one should keep from a wicked man cannot be measured.
20. Large desire is endless poverty.

21. Only mad dogs and Englishmen go out in noonday sun.
22. Separation secure manifest friendship.
23. September blow soft till the fruit's in the loft.
24. Sit on the bank of the river and wait; your enemy's corpse will soon float by.
25. The way to overcome the angry man is with gentleness, the evil man with goodness, the miser with generosity and liar with truth.
26. The weakest go to the wall.
27. You can often find in rivers what you cannot find in oceans.
28. You can only lean against that which resist.
29. If you live in the river you should make friends with the crocodiles.
30. When you were born, you cried and the world rejoiced. Live your life so that when you die, the world cries and you rejoiced.
31. The first day a guest, the second day guest, the third day a calamity.
32. There is nothing noble in being superior to some other person. True nobility is in superior to your previous self.
33. Non violence is the supreme law of life.
34. The most beautiful things in the universe are the starry heavens above us and the feeling of duty with us.
35. Call on God, but row away from the rock.
36. A guilty conscience is a hidden enemy.
37. Be first at the feast and last at the fight.
38. Do not blame God for having created the tiger, but thank him for not having given it wings.

39. I have lanced many boils, but none pained like my own.
40. If we did precious things from the land, we will invite disaster.
41. Nothing is comprehensible except by virtue of its edges.
42. One "no" averts seventy evils.
43. Pray one hour before going to war, two hours before going to sea and three hours before getting married.
44. The sieve says to the needle, you have a hole in your head.
45. The tree casts its shade upon all, even the woodcutter.
46. There no evil without its advantage.
47. Those who hunt deer sometimes raise tigers.
48. To lend is to buy a quarrel.
49. Under the mountain is silver and gold, but under the night sky, hunger and cold.
50. When you are in the water you swim.
51. Children are poor man's riches.
52. Do not look where you fell, but were you slipped.

Indian (Hindi)

1. Self praise is no praise.
2. The young crow is wiser than its mother.
3. What is the play to one is death to another.
4. In a treeless country, the castor-oil plan is a big.
5. A scalded cat dreads cold water.
6. I am king; you are a king, who is to fetch water?
7. Too lose is to learn.
8. Can your hands do what you're your tongue does?
9. To lend is buy a quarrel.
10. He who will not climb will not fall.
11. Man is his own devil.
12. On a green tree there are many parrots.
13. God gives food to every bird, but does no throw it into the nest.
14. The washer man never tears his father's clothes.
15. A fool went to fish, but lost his fishing basket.
16. The eyes do not see what the mind does not want.
17. Don't bargain for fish which are in still in the water.
18. A thief is a thief, whether he steals a diamond or a cucumber.
19. God takes care of a blind cow.
20. One who cannot dance blames the floor.
21. Call on God, but row away from the rocks.

Indonesian
1. Where there is sugar there are ants.
2. There is a shrimp behind the stone.
3. Water with ripple is shallow.
4. Water dripping from the roof will eventually go to the reservoir.
5. Water minced will not separate.
6. Milk is repaid with poison.
7. The child in the lap is let go, a monkey from the forest is nursed instead.
8. The dogs are barking, the caravan moves on.
9. Where there is shit, there are flies.
10. Like the bamboo and the river bank.
11. If you enter a goat stable, bleat if you enter water buffalo stable bellow.
12. Ripping water shows lack of depth.
13. The shadow should be the same length as the body.
14. The shallower the brook, the more babbles.
15. An elephant that dies leave its tusks, a tiger that dies leaves its stripes, a person who dies leave his/her name (legacy).
16. The will of the heart is to hug the mountain but the arm is not long enough.

Iranian

1. Epigram succeed where epic fail.
2. It is nothing for one to know something unless another knows you know it.
3. Go and wake up your luck.
4. Do well the little thing now, so shall great things come to thee by and by asking to be done.
5. Every man goes down to his death bearing in his hands only that which he has given away.

Irish

1. A hair on the head is worth two on the brush.
2. A kind word never broke anyone's mouth.
3. A lie travels farther than the truth.
4. A light heart lives long.
5. A silent mouth is sweet to hear.
6. A turkey never voted for an early Christmas.
7. Better be quarrelling than lonesome.
8. Bricks and mortar makes a house, but laughter of children makes home.
9. Do not break your shin on a stool that is not in your way.
10. Even the longest day has its end.
11. Give away all you like, but keep your bills and your temper.
12. Good luck beats early rising.
13. If you dig a grave for others you might fall into it yourself.
14. If you get a reputation as an early riser, you can sleep till noon.
15. It's no use carrying an umbrella if your shoes are not leaking.
16. Praise the young and they will flourish.
17. Praise the youth and it will prosper.
18. The believer is happy, the doubter is wise.
19. You've got to do your own growing, no matter how tall your grandfather was.
20. The longest road out is the shortest road home.
21. The older the fiddle the sweeter the tune.
22. There is no need to fear the wind if your haystacks are tied down.
23. Do not mistake a goat beard for a fine stallion tail.

24. Drink is the curse of the land – it makes you fight with your neighbour.
25. If you lie down with dogs you will rise with fleas.
26. A wild goose never reared a tame gosling.
27. A boy best friend is his mother and there is no spancel stronger than her apron string.
28. A trout in the pot is better than a salmon in the sea.
29. A narrow neck keeps the bottle from being emptied in one swing.
30. The best way to keep loyalty in a man's heart is to keep money in his purse.
31. If the knitter is weary the baby will have no new bonnet.
32. Even a tin knocker will shine on dirty floor.
33. An old broom knows the dirty corner best.
34. One beetle recognizes another.
35. To a raven its own chick is white.
36. Any man can lose his hat in a fairy wind.
37. If you have one pair of good soles it's better than two pairs of good uppers.
38. It is difficult to choose between two blind goats.
39. A silent mouth is sweet to hear.
40. It's bad hen that won't scratch itself.
41. A nod is as good as a wink to a blind horse.
42. The fox never found a better messenger than itself.
43. Show the fatted calf but not the things that fatted it.
44. In winter the milk goes to the cow's horns.
45. Men are like bagpipes no sound comes from them until they are full.

46. Snuff at a wake is fine there is nobody sneezing over the snuff box.
47. You must crack the nut before you can eat the kernel.
48. He got it from nature as the pig got the rooting in the ground.
49. Often a cow does not take after its breed.
50. If you put a silk dress on a goat it is goat still.
51. What is in the marrow is hard to take out of the bone.
52. The wood will renew the foliage its sheds.
53. What will come from the briar but the berry?
54. One who is without cows must be his own dog.
55. A blind man can see his mouth.
56. A king's son is not nobler than his food.
57. Keep your tongue in your jaw and your tow in your pump.
58. Pity the man who has a stranger's spancel on him.
59. To every cow its calf, to every book its copy.
60. Watching is part of good play.
61. Patience cure many an old complaint.
62. The one, who waits the fine day, will get the fine day.
63. Patience and forbearance makes a bishop of his reverence.
64. When apple is ripe it will fall.
65. Patience can conquer destiny.
66. Patience is a plaster for all sores.
67. For what cannot be cured patience is the best.
68. There is no tree heaven higher than the tree of patience.
69. Patience is a virtue that causes no shame.

70. Time and patience would bring the snail to Jerusalem.
71. Everyone praises the native land.
72. Nobody ever brought peace, the man who hadn't got it; peace (quietness) is worth buying.
73. The world is quite and the pig is in the sky.
74. To the fighting man peace is sure.
75. The end of the feast is better than the beginning of a fight.
76. An eye is blind in another man's corner.
77. He is more to be pitied than laughed at.

Italian

1. A cat pent up becomes a lion.
2. A favour to come is better than a hundred received.
3. A runaway monk never praises his monastery.
4. A woman, a steak and a walnut tree, the more they are beaten the better they better.
5. Anger can be an expensive luxury.
6. At a dangerous passage, yield to precedence.
7. Better a mouse in the pot than no flesh at all.
8. Better give a penny then lend twenty.
9. Between saying and doing many pair of shoes is worn out.
10. Chose neither a woman nor linen by candlelight.
11. Everyone loves justice in the affairs of another.
12. For a wife and horse to your neighbour.
13. Give neither counsel nor salt till you are asked for it.
14. Half brain is enough for him who says little.
15. Have an open face but conceal your thoughts.
16. He that marries a widow with four children marries four thieves.
17. He who begins many things finishes few.
18. He who wants great deal must not ask for little.
19. He would share even his share of the sun.
20. High birth is a poor dish at table.
21. If the patient dies, the doctor has killed him, but if he gets well the saints have saved him.
22. I'm buying a horse and taking a wife, shut your eyes and commend yourself to God.
23. In prosperity no alters smoke.
24. Land was never lost for want of an heir.

25. Love is an excuse for its own faults.
26. No pears fall into a shut mouth.
27. One may have good eyes and yet see nothing.
28. Praise a maid in the morning and the weather at night.
29. She who is born a beauty is born betrothed.
30. Silence was never written down.
31. Teeth placed before the tongue, give good advice.
32. Tell not all you know, believe not all you hear, do not all you are able.
33. The comforter's head never aches.
34. The ropes of lawyers are lined with obstinacy of suitors.
35. There is no need to bind up one's head before it is broken.
36. Those who have fine clothes in their chest can wear rags.
37. To a covered ill an open razor.
38. Trifles make perfection, but perfection is not trifle.
39. Trouble rides a fast horse.
40. What does not poison fattens.
41. When ill luck falls asleep, let none wake her.
42. When the sun is the highest cast the least shadow.
43. Who gives bread to other's dogs is often barked at by its own.
44. Who offends write on sand, who is offended on marble.
45. Who sow thorns should not go barefoot.
46. With so many roosters crowing the sun never comes up.

47. Write down the advice of him who loves you, though you like it or not at present.

Jamaica

1. The higher the monkey climbs the more it exposed.
2. Hear no evil, see no evil.
3. Where there is too much merriment and excitement danger lurks near.
4. When things and times are the hardest brighter times are nearer.
5. If you survive unharmed, everything is fine.
6. If an experience does not destroy you, you can benefit greatly from it.
7. Make use of the first opportunity.
8. If you are in sheltered situation, you don't know what hardships are.
9. Don't be someone you are not.
10. If you want it done right, do it yourself.
11. Stone at the bottom of the river do not know how hot the sun is.
12. Roach (cockroaches) must not get involved in chicken fight.
13. Cows have no business in horseplay.
14. If you saw what the river carried, you would never drink the water.
15. Keep your secret in your own gourdy.
16. Keep your shop and your shop will keep you.
17. Make a friend when you don't need one.
18. No call alligator long mouth till you pass him.
19. Sleep has no master.
20. Those who can't dance say the music is no good.
21. Words in mouth, no loud upon head.
22. You shake man's hand, you shake his heart.

23. When you reach out a hand good things come back to you.
24. To walk is better than to sit down.
25. Children (or anyone) who don't hear (don't take) good advice (hard ear) will encounter great hardship.
26. A hungry man cannot work.
27. Good manner take you through the world.
28. Everything has its usefulness.
29. As long as someone is alive don't dismiss their potentials.
30. One shouldn't belittle someone who is like them is some ways.
31. You can't turn back the hand of time.
32. What you see on the outside doesn't mean it's the same on the inside.
33. Don't care how much disguise someone puts on their true self will surface.
34. A new broom sweeps clean, but an old broom knows every corner.
35. Bad luck is worse than witchcraft.
36. Words die and men keep on living.

Jewish

1. A bird that you set free may be caught again, but a word that escapes your lips will not return.
2. A mother understands what a child does not say.
3. A pessimist confronted with two bad choices, choose both.
4. As he thinks in his heart so he is.
5. As you teach, you learn.
6. Ask about your neighbour then buy the house.
7. Do not be wise in words –be wise in deeds.
8. Don't be sweet, lest you be eaten up, don't be bitter lest you be spewed out.
9. Don't live in town were there are no doctors.
10. Don't look for more honour than your learning merits.
11. He that can't endure bad, will not live to see the good.
12. If charity cost nothing, the world will be full of philanthropists.
13. If God lived on earth, people would break his windows.
14. If not for fear, sin would be sweet.
15. If the rich could hire the poor to die for them, the poor would make a very nice living.
16. Make sure to be in with your equals if you are going to fall out with your supervisor.
17. Not to have felt the pain is not to have been human.
18. Rejoice not in thine enemy's fall-but don't rush to pick him up either.
19. What you don't see with your eyes don't invent with your mouth.

20. Worries go down better with soup than without.
21. Half truth is a whole lie.
22. Among those who stand do not sit, among those who sit do not stand. Among those who laugh, do not weep, among those who weep, do not laugh.
23. Anyone who teases you, love you.
24. Ask about your neighbor and then buy the house.
25. Be sure to send a lazy man for the angel of death.
26. Be the day weary or be the day long, at last it ringeth to evensong.
27. Do not make yourself too big, you are not so small.
28. Do not meet trouble half way.
29. Don't look a gift horse in the mouth.
30. Don't make a mountain out of a molehill.
31. Don't make toil of pleasure.
32. Don't open a shop unless you know how to smile.
33. Don't pick a wasp out of a cream-jug.
34. God could not be everywhere and therefore he made mothers.
35. God give burden also shoulders.
36. He who puts up insult invites injuries.
37. If you can't get over you must go under.
38. In a restaurant choose a table near a waiter.
39. Look for good, not the evil, in the conduct of members of the family.
40. Never trust people who tell you all their troubles but keep you from all their joys.
41. Prepare your proof before you argue.
42. Pride is the mask of one's own faults.
43. Pride that dined with vanity supped with poverty.

44. The inner keeper loves drunkards but not for a son in law.
45. The only true deeds are those who have been forgotten.
46. What you give for the cause of charity in health is gold, what you give in sickness is silver, what you give after death is lead.
47. When two divorced people marry, four people get into bed.
48. When you have no choices mobilize the spirit of courage.
49. With money in your pocket you are wise, you are handsome and you sing well too.
50. You can't force anyone to love you or lend you money
51. Your friend has a friend, don't tell him.
52. God is close to those with broken heart.
53. Loneliness breaks the spirit.
54. What soap is for the body tears are for the soul?
55. I ask not for lighter burden, but for broader shoulder.
56. Against stupidity, God himself is helpless.
57. People come to poverty in two ways, accumulating debt and paying them off.
58. Truth is the safest lie.
59. Just as courage imperils life, fear protects it.
60. God created one world full of small worlds.
61. The sun will sets today without your assistance.
62. Do not speak of secrets in a field that is full of little hills.
63. The longer the blind man lives the more he sees.
64. A coin in an empty barrel makes a lot of noise.

65. Don't approach a goat from front, a horse from the back or a fool from any side.
66. He is not called wise who know good and ill, but he who can recognize the two evils the lesser.
67. Opinions founded on prejudiced are always sustained with the greatest violence.

Kashmiri

1. One person's vomit is another's food.
2. One man can burn water, whereas another cannot even burn oil.
3. I brought the nettle, sawed the nettle, and then the nettle stung me.
4. One man's beard is on fire, and another man warm his hand on it.
5. A king for a moment, and a beggar soon after.
6. To eat out of vessel and then defile it.
7. To show one's fist to a blind man is neither a sin nor virtue.
8. Advice is lost on stupid people.
9. All people came (were born) in good health, but none left (died) healthy.
10. A relative remains relative, as long as relations are maintained.
11. God take care of our handicaps.
12. Leftovers of others could be a hearty meal for others.
13. Being exceptionally lucky it is applicable to persons who are in the right situation at the right time.
14. The path to heart lies through one's stomach.
15. A small stone can be hidden under a big one.
16. The child who is not afraid of anyone is like a Horse without a bridle.
17. An idle person has three tasks: sleeping, eating and quarrelling.
18. Only wearer knows where the shoe pinches.
19. The hungry should not be taken to a feast, and a naked person should not be taken to a cloth shop.
20. The fall is nobody's desire.
21. As long as one is rich, one commands.

22. Distance lends enchantment and familiarity breeds contempt.
23. No strength within, no respect without.
24. One and one are sometimes eleven.

Kenya

1. Love your enemy.
2. However much it rains on you no wild banana tree will grow on your head.
3. Promise is debt.
4. Who thinks to stay should take care not to fall.
5. Knowledge is power.
6. Intelligence is like hair, everyone has its own.
7. What the mother does no teach will be taught by the world.
8. Who does not hear most not feel.
9. The retailer does not argue.
10. Good things sell, bad things advertise.
11. A sinking ship depletes a jar of honey.
12. The sign for rain are the clouds.
13. Blood is thicker than water.
14. A tool to fight fire is fire.
15. An empty pot makes the loudest noise.
16. The curse of the Fowl does not bother the Eagle.
17. Your profit is my loss.
18. The stick in the hand kills the Snake.
19. Dip after dip depletes a jar of honey.
20. A slave has no choice.
21. How easy it is to defeat people who do not kindle fire for themselves.
22. How gentle glides the married life away, when she who rules still seems but to obey.
23. Having good discussion is like having riches.
24. He who does not know one thing knows another.
25. All cassavas have the same skin but not all taste the same.
26. A person changing his clothing always hides while changing.
27. You may laugh at a friend's roof, don't laugh at his sleeping accommodation.

28. We have not inherited this land from our ancestors; rather we have borrowed it from our children.
29. He who is unable to dance says the yard is stony.
30. Nobody gathers firewood to roast a thin Goat.
31. Those who get to the river early drink the cleanest water.
32. Many births mean many burials.
33. The important things are left in the locker.
34. A boy isn't send to collect the honey.
35. Blind belief is dangerous.
36. Hurrying has no blessing.
37. A Donkey always says thank you with a kick.
38. A messenger cannot be beaten.
39. A dog that steals sells its body.
40. A champion bulls starts from birth.
41. No water without waves.
42. No length without end.
43. It is better for the eye to die than the heart.
44. A willing hand makes work easy.
45. If you do not know death, look at the grave.
46. To celebrate does not last forever.
47. Ignorance is like a dark night.
48. A good name shines in the dark.
49. A rope parts where thinnest (Blame is always fall on the weak)
50. Many hands make work easy.
51. Cut your nose to save your face.
52. One finger does not kill a Louse.
53. Truth is stronger than weapon.
54. What bite you is in your clothes (the enemy is among us)
55. Every ship has its own waves.
56. Every door has its own key.
57. Every Bird files with its own wings.
58. Getting is not cleverness, lacking is not stupidity.
59. Hard times do not preclude good times.

Khakas

1. Horses become acquainted by neighing and people by talking.
2. An autumn day feeds a whole winter.
3. The hurrying fly falls into the milk.
4. Haste makes waste.
5. Every Fox praises its (own) tail
6. Learning is better than becoming rich.
7. A fearful person even fears the Hare.
8. Moss grows on a lying stone.
9. Seven people do not wait for person.

Korean

1. Where a tiger dies, it leaves its leather behind.
2. Even a dog can recite poetry.
3. After losing a cow, one repairs the barn.
4. An empty cart rattles louder.
5. Gather dust to build a mountain.
6. It's darkest underneath the lamp stand.
7. Even a sheet of paper seems lighter when two people lift it together.
8. Don't try to cover the whole sky with the palm of your hand.
9. A kitchen knife cannot carve it's own handle.
10. A noble man's calf does not know how a butcher kills.
11. Carve the peg by looking at the hole.
12. Cast no dirt into the well that gives you water.
13. Cast no pearl to swine.
14. Cast not a shadow, and lose substance.
15. Cross even a stone bridge after you have tested it.
16. Even a fish wouldn't get into trouble if it kept its mouth shut.
17. Even children of the same mother look different.
18. If there is a rich man is the area three villages are ruined.
19. If you starve for three days, there is no thought that does not invade your imagination.
20. Man's affairs are evaluated only after his coffin is closed.
21. Man's extremity God's opportunity.
22. Put off one day and ten day will pass.
23. The bad plod man quarrels with his Ox.
24. The deeper the water are, the more still they run.

25. Where there are no tigers, a wildcat is very self-important.
26. Words have no wings but they can fly a thousand miles.
27. You will hate a beautiful song if you sing it often.
28. A turtle travels only when it sticks its neck out.
29. Power last years, influence not more than a hundred.
30. Starting is half the task.
31. Even if the sky falls on you, there is a hole; there is a hole that you can escape from.

Kurdish

1. A visitor comes with ten blessing, eats one and leaves nine.
2. Do not throw the arrows which will return against you.
3. Fear an ignorant man more than a Lion.
4. For every wise man there is one still wiser.
5. Give nine, save seven.
6. Guests bring good luck with them.
7. Habit becomes second nature.
8. In a flat country a hillock thinks itself a mountain.
9. It is easier to make a camel jump a ditch than to make fool listen to reason.
10. It is more difficult to contend with oneself than with the world.
11. Kind's words will unlock an iron door.
12. Listen a hundred times, ponder a thousand times, speak once.
13. Many will show you the way once your cart has overturned.
14. Many women, many words.
15. No matter where you go, your destiny follows you.
16. No means, no market.
17. Of everything else the newest, of friends, the oldest.
18. Of evil grain no good seed can come.
19. Once a friend always friend.
20. One beats one's break who does not beat one's child.
21. Part with your head, but not with your heart.
22. Parting is such a sweet sorrow.
23. See with your mind, hear with your heart.
24. Stairs are climbed step by step.

25. The devil tempts all, but the idle mind tempts the devil.
26. The devil takes a hand in what is done in haste.
27. What you give away you keep.
28. When a cat wants to eat her Kitten, she says they look like a Mice.
29. If you do not contribute positively, least do not contribute adversity.
30. If you are not a rose, do not be a thorn either.
31. Whatever your heart thinks, your mouth speaks.
32. The distance between of 1000 mile begins with one step.
33. The fox did not reach the grape, said it's unripe.
34. Help yourself and be love by others.
35. A lion is a lion, whether male or female.
36. One who has a little wisdom will have greater burden.
37. Light wisdom heavy burden.
38. Search yourself and you will find Allah.
39. A tribulation is better than hundred warning.

Latin

1. By learning you will teach, by teaching you will understand.
2. The king is from God, the law is from the king.
3. From thing's possibility one cannot be certain of its reality.
4. He who quarrels with a drunk hurts an absentee.
5. Abuse no argument against proper use.
6. What happened were a story / fable.
7. To high places by narrow roads.
8. No one is obliged to do impossible.
9. Add little to little and there will be a big pile.
10. As long as a sick person is conscious, there is still hope.
11. A friend is another self.
12. A true friend is a discerned during an uncertain matter.
13. A great friend is the greatest treasure in life.
14. Love of the fatherland is our law.
15. True friend becomes known in the love, the disposition, the speeches, the deeds.
16. The eagle does not hurt flies.
17. you acquire what you reap
18. Art is to conceal art.
19. Art is long, life is short.
20. Gold is power.
21. Fortunes favour the brave.
22. Hear, see, and be silent, if you wish to live (in peace).
23. The other part should be heard as well.
24. The accursed hunger for gold.
25. Dawn is a friend of muses.
26. Either learn or leave.
27. I will either find a way or I will make one.
28. He is lucky who helps everyone he can.

29. He is lucky the one who gets an advantage from those on which he has some power.
30. Let war pay for itself.
31. Something that is well diagnosed can be cured well.
32. He lives well who lives unnoticed
33. Repetitions are not well received.
34. Good health is worth more than the greatest wealth
35. A good Sheppard shears his sheep, he doesn't flay them.
36. If Caesar where alive, you would be chained to an oar.
37. Let the buyer beware.
38. Hunger is a spice for any good meal.
39. Clear agreements, good friends.
40. Shut your mouth, open your eyes.
41. Harmony of citizens is the wall of cities.
42. Well-being through harmony.
43. The power of habit is great.
44. Habit is second nature.
45. There is no herb against power of death.
46. Opposites are cured by their opposites.
47. The greater the degeneration of the republic, the more of its laws.
48. I believe it because it is absurd.
49. It is crueller to be always afraid of dying than to die.
50. Every human can make mistake.
51. Any man can make a mistake, only a fool keep on making the same one.
52. Fool me once and shame on you, fool me twice and shame on me
53. Patience is the cure of all sufferings.
54. If you live properly, don't worry about what the evil ones say.

55. Cure thyself.
56. The pious are (in) the care of gods.
57. They condemn what they do not understand.
58. In the matter of taste there is no dispute.
59. The authority (or king or law) does not care about trivial things.
60. Of the dead, nothing but good.
61. Offence to the gods is the concern of the goods.
62. They created desolation and they call it peace.
63. The woman, beautiful above, ends in a Fish.
64. The said is nothing for the wise.
65. It is hard not to write satire.
66. Divide and govern.
67. I give that you may give.
68. We learn by teaching.
69. As long as you are prosperous (wealthy), you will have many friends.
70. It is the dose that makes the poison.
71. Never tickle a sleeping Dragon.
72. Lead by example.
73. The name "peace" is sweet itself.
74. It is sweet and honourable to die for the fatherland.
75. As long as I breathe, I hope.
76. Where life is, hope is.
77. Living, I was mute, dead, I sweetly sing.
78. When two do the same, it isn't the same.
79. While two men argue, the third one rejoices.
80. The law is harsh, but it is the law.
81. Necessity is harsh.
82. The tree can be recognised by its fruits.
83. Out of many, one.
84. To be is to be perceived.
85. To be rather than to seem.
86. To err is human; to repeat is of the devil.
87. And acknowledge itself is power.

88. And now king, be warned, you who judge on earth.
89. Events are the teacher of a stupid person.
90. From the abundance of the heart, the mouth speaks.
91. From stars, to knowledge.
92. From power, truth.
93. Nothing comes from nothing.
94. Life is more than merely staying alive.
95. Misuse does not nullify proper use.
96. He calls hell.
97. Eggs today are better than chickens tomorrow.
98. Don't speak against the sun.
99. The disease worsens, with treatment.
100. A precipice in front, wolves behind.
101. The deepest river flow with the least sound.
102. Even a God find it hard to love and be wise at the same time.
103. Lovers are lunatics.
104. Lovers' quarrels are the renewal of love.
105. The ass rubs the ass.
106. Fortune favours the bold.
107. Either to conquer or to die.
108. Hail, Caesar, we who are about to die salute you.
109. Blessed are those who possess possessions in nine points of the law.
110. To accept favours is to sell one's freedom.
111. Good wind gladdens a person's heart.
112. Seize the day.
113. Beware of what you say, when and to whom.
114. May he love tomorrow who has never looked before, and may he who has loved, love tomorrow as well.
115. Slight grief talk, great ones are speechless.
116. Of two evil, the lesser is always to be chosen.

117. A praetor does not occupy himself with petty matters.
118. As long as you are fortunate, you will have many friends.
119. The law is hard, but it is the law.
120. I have raised a monument more durable than bronze.
121. The result validates the deeds.
122. Hunger sweetens the beans.
123. Resolutely in action, gentle in a manner.
124. In peace, like wise man, he appropriately prepares for war.
125. It is fitting that a liar should be a man of good memory.
126. A sound mind in a sound body.
127. No one is free who is slave to his body.
128. Life is not being alive but being well.
129. Not for you, not for me, but for us.
130. It will not always be summer.
131. Small things occupy light minds.
132. All thing change, and we change with them.
133. Mountain will be in labour, and an absurd mouse will be born.
134. Flatters are the worst type of enemies.
135. The can because they seem to be able.
136. Rather to die than to be dishonoured.
137. Forewarned is forearmed.
138. It is human nature to hate a person whom you have injures.
139. Whom the gods love dies young.
140. He who writes read twice something to keep in mind when developing web pages.
141. The love of money is root of all evil.
142. Examine the past, examine the present, and examine the future.
143. Let the superior answer.

144. A wise man states a true nothing he does not prove.
145. If you did it, deny it.
146. If the end is good, everything will be good.
147. If glory comes after death, I am not in a hurry
148. Chalk is the pen of fools.
149. Let not your spending exceeds your income.
150. Yield not your misfortunes, but advance all the more boldly against them.
151. Safety for the vanquished is to abadon hope of safety knowing there is no hope that can give one the courage to fight and win.
152. I came, I saw, I conquered himself.
153. Conquers who conquers himself.
154. That man is wise who talks little.
155. By learning you teach, by teaching you learn.
156. If the wind will not serve, take oars.
157. It is honourable to be accused by those who deserved to be accused.
158. It is part of a good Sheppard to shear his flock, not to skin it.
159. Never give a child a sword.
160. Hay is more acceptable to an ass than gold.

Lebanese

1. He who has money can eat sherbet in hell.
2. His brain hang at the top of his fez
3. If anyone is not willing to accept your point of view, try to see his point of view.
4. If at first you don't succeed, try, try, and try again.
5. Lock your door rather than accuse your neighbour.
6. Lower your voice and strengthen your argument.
7. The worst ache is the present ache
8. We traded in shrouds, people stopped dying.

Liberia

1. Do not look where you fell, but where you slipped.
2. If the towns' people are happy, look for the chief.
3. If the wall were adamant, gold would take the town.
4. He who knows the way must conduct others.
5. When pointing an evil finger at a man, three fingers at a man, three fingers are pointing at you.
6. The stone that you throw into the well to kill frog are the same stones that will cause you to suffer when drinking the dirty water.
7. He who steps in (arrive) first shows the depth of the current.
8. To cure a bad sore, you must use bad medicine.
9. The leaf that is very sweet in a goat's mouth sometimes hurts his stomach.
10. A man cannot be taller than his head
11. Washing with dirty water does not clean a dirty object.
12. A curled snake never gets fat.
13. A little rain each day wills the river overflowing.
14. Do not eat your chicken and throw its feathers in the front yard.
15. Good millet is known at the harvest.
16. Only when the tree is big and strong can you tether a cow to it.
17. Through the palm tree in the jungle is big, who knows how big its yield will be.
18. To the patient man will come all the riches of the world?
19. When building a house, don't measure the timbers in the forest.

Macedonia

1. What one fool can ensnare, not a thousand sages can fix.
2. Think twice, say once.
3. Feed a dog to bark at you.
4. A good friend is recognised in times of trouble.
5. Where force rules, justice does not exist.
6. The brain is not in the pocket, but in the head.
7. Brother does not feed his brother but it is hard not having one
8. Lie bread so I can eat you.

Malagasy

1. Words are like eggs. When they are hatched, they have wings.
2. Words are like new hatched eggs, they already have wings.
3. Words are like spider web, a shelter for the clever one and a trap for the not so clever.
4. Words go further than bullets.

Malaysian (Malay)

1. Do not think that placid water is without Crocodiles.
2. No matter how high the squirrel jumps, it will eventually fall into the ground.
3. Smart people do not make mistakes at times.
4. After falling, the ladder falls upon you.
5. Tigers die leaving their stripes (of their fur) but humans dies leaving their names.
6. Being grateful early will be advantageous, being regretful later is of no use.
7. Bit by bit, in the end it comes a hill.
8. Like peanuts, who forgets its shell?
9. Mike belongs to the cow, but the bull cow gets the name.
10. A fool is like a big drum beats fast bust doesn't realise its hollowness.
11. An ox with long horns, even if he does not but, will be accused of butting.
12. An unmasked excuse infers transgression.
13. Ants die in sugar.
14. Clapping with one hand only will not produce a noise.
15. If the is no reason, why would the tempura bird nest on the low branches.
16. If you have, give it, if you lack seek.
17. One can pay back the loan of gold, but one dies forever in debt to those who are kind.
18. Smack a tray of water an you get to wash your face.
19. The existence of the sea means the existence of pirates.
20. The more shoots, the more leaves.
21. The more sorrow, one encounters, the more joy one can contain.
22. To bend a bamboo, start when it is a shoot.
23. Where there is sugar, there are bonds to be the ants.

24. You can't get at the precious sago without first breaking the bark.
25. Like a candle, burning itself to light the people.
26. Hear from the right ear, out from the left ear.
27. Whoever eats chill gets burned.
28. Sun for the year is wiped out by rain for a day.
29. If you chop water, it won't separate.
30. Banana plant does not bear fruits twice.
31. If there is no rattan, roots will do.
32. Friends to laugh with are many; friends to cry with are few.
33. We have the same black hair, but hair, but not the heart.
34. Like an enemy hiding under your blanket.
35. The language you speak would tell us your race.
36. Don't try to teach a duck how to swim.
37. Drink water while you swim.
38. A Turtle lays thousands of eggs, nobody knows, but a when a hen lays an egg, the whole village know.
39. Just like a crab, teaching its young how to walk straight.
40. Talk doesn't cook rice.
41. If you are reluctant to ask the way, you will be lost.

Manx

1. Cheerfulness with an empty pocket is better than discontent with a full one.
2. A friend by thee is better than a brother far off.
3. The coroner and the lawyer grow fat on the quarrel of fools.
4. Better leave something to an enemy than borrow from friends.
5. What must be, will.
6. A man that's poor, let him be poor forever and whoever has little, give him little.
7. Thou art promising me the birds, but I must catch them myself.
8. The more on the tally, the heavier the payment.
9. It will come to us if we will wait long enough.
10. Take thy time, it will come to thee.
11. It is easy to bake where there is plenty of meal.
12. There is a skeleton in every cupboard.
13. An eel by his tail, an Irishman at his word.
14. Marry for love, and work for money, but yet be sure not to love where there is none.
15. Never marry a woman unless you can see the smoke of her father's chimney from your maddens.
16. Thrifty fingers are better than a marriage march.
17. A slow fire makes sweet Malt.
18. When the sun shines is the time to make up hay.
19. Praise the fun day in the evening.
20. As the day lengthens, the cold strengthens.
21. When the moon rises before day, it often makes the night better.
22. The blighting east wind destroys everything.
23. Rain is the mother of wind.
24. After rain will come drought, after storm will come calm.
25. When the wind blow the sea is moving.

26. When the Frog spawn in the middle of the pool, it is a sign of a dry spring, when they spawn in the side of the pool, it is a sign of a wet spring.
27. Winter thunders, summer wonders.
28. A wet Christmas, a fat churchyard.
29. Sunlight is the best light in Ireland.
30. At Candlemas day, half fodder half firing.
31. The weakness of old age are not fit cause for laughter, since they must be own portion at the end.
32. A man in love is a fool, an old man in love is the greatest fool of all through their vanity in being trusted with them, do not trust any with them if you are able to avoid it.
33. While seeking new friends, hold to the old.
34. Choose him for a friend who incites you to good works.
35. The remembrance of the heart is better than the remembrance of the head.
36. Think highly of your friends for perhaps they may not be long with you.
37. Never part with those you love without loving words, perhaps you will not meet them again.
38. He tells you the fault of the others will tell your faults to them.
39. He who seeks for a friend with a fault can never find him.
40. The money we are dealing with we may lose, but our treasure in heaven will be in safety.
41. A rich man without liberality is like a tree without fruits.
42. Better be remembered in prayer of good man than in the will of a rich man.
43. Better be poor and honest than to be rich and d lying.
44. It is not what we, take up, but what we give up that make us rich.
45. The more on the tally the more the pay.

46. Foolish spending is the father of poverty.
47. The man who looks after his own work has plenty to do keep everything right.
48. If you would grow poor without knowing it, put your helper to work and go to sleep.
49. He who does more today than usual designs to deceive you or fail.
50. Begin not the day's work without breaking thy fast.
51. It is more difficult to begin at the third hour than at the first hour.
52. A man that is not wise in his works is not wise in his faith.
53. When man are rightly occupied their happiness grows of their work.
54. Labour and wait, time ripens the corn, but will not plough the fields.
55. The woman who puts a bridle on her tongue does not make much mischief.
56. Simplicity is the beauty of a woman.
57. You will know a bad girl by her impudent eye, keep her under and don't give her too much liberty, or she will bring you to shame.
58. A woman's love and her trust are written in dust they will fail.
59. Happy is the bride the sun shines on.
60. Blessed is the man who has a wife of his own.
61. Marry a woman and then try how you will get done with her.
62. A woman who seeks society of other men does not think much of her own husband.
63. A man that is married has lost all his hope, he is just like a pig with his leg in a rope.
64. A dark night is the best time to go a courting.
65. There is not much happiness for a man who is in the world alone.
66. Blessed are they who are born females.

67. The best way to remember God is to forget yourself.
68. If the devil has rocked you to sleep ask God to turn over the cradle.
69. Desire to do right and God will give you the grace to do right.
70. To believe God is the holiest wisdom.
71. No man can praise God while he steals from his neighbour.
72. The man that is right with God will do right with God.
73. Where God's grace cannot keep you, his providence has not sent you.
74. Be one of God's windows that His glory may shine through.
75. God has put the church in the world; the devil has put the world in the church.
76. The right love is to hate that which destroys the soul.
77. The truth that dwells within you will shine out in your life.
78. A man that is not a saint for speaking saint's words.
79. Joseph's steadfastness in righteousness raised him to the throne.
80. Faith saves us, but assurance satisfies.
81. Sin trample under foot makes a ladder to heaven.
82. The only holy waters are the cup of cold water.
83. Man at his wit's end is not at the end of his faith.
84. Do not toll the bell for prayer and then runaway.
85. Se the dial of your heart by the sun of righteousness.
86. Prayer in the morning opens the gate of duty for the day.
87. Your first care must be the care of your heart.
88. You cannot plug the fruit of happiness from the tree of unrighteousness.
89. The wisdom of the world is the best tools for the devil.
90. Put off the old man and do not cloth him with a new garment.

91. Fear nothing but unbelief.
92. The windows of heaven turn on the hinges of love.
93. It is only when sin is dead that we begin to leave.
94. Sins destroy nothing but the place where it reigns.
95. Prayer is the vessel in which we carry water from the rock.
96. One sin doer not saves from another.
97. The preacher who makes sport to men is a destroyer of souls.
98. Justice wrongs no man.
99. No man can do much harm to your good name but yourself.
100. As you hope to be born with yourself, bear with other people.
101. When the well runs dry we know what it is to want water.
102. A gossip's mouth is the devil's post-bag.
103. If the people do what which is right earnestly, in time it will be a pleasure to them.
104. The greatest pleasure in life lies in doing that which people say we cannot do.
105. A man should not be ashamed to acknowledge his fault.
106. When he is wrong, what is it but saying in other words that he is wiser today than he was yesterday.
107. Many men many minds.
108. The bitter cup we strive to remove from us hold the medicine we are in need of.
109. To sin against the law is boldness, but to sin against love is hateful.
110. When a man cuts for himself he often cuts his own finger.
111. Suffer wrong with meekness, everyone of the shall be made right in eternity.
112. Our greatest danger lies hidden in little things.

113.Many a man has been guarding the bush and another plucking the fruit.
114.Where there are geese there is dirt, and where there women there is talking.
115.The well-fed never felt like ill-fed.
116.It is the cow that calls most which gives most milk.
117.The black ox never trod on his own foot.
118.None is deaf as the one who will not hear.
119.Partner in work, partner in food.
120.Give piece to the raven and he will be back.
121.Between two stools, your arse is on the floor.
122.He who acknowledges no judge condemns himself.
123.He who is harmed shall be mocked.
124.A man who gets a good man to marry his daughter gains son, but a man who gets a bad son-in-law also loses a daughter.
125. Bought wit is the best wit, if it is not too expensive.
126.A big head of the smallest with and a little head with none at all, use it to measure sense.
127.If customs are not customary, custom will mourn.
128.The smaller the company, the better the share, the bigger the company, the merrier the play.
129.The nearer the bone, the sweeter the flesh.
130.Plough the patches you missed to make the good earth.
131.There is a great difference between the just and the unjust.
132.Crooked bannock, straight belly.
133.They are living hitting the cat and a dog.
134.They are shaking their pride on each other.
135.There is a bigger wrinkle in your arse than before.
136.Shameful leftovers are worse than disgraceful eating.
137.There are many turns in the marriage tune.
138.The little hemlock is a sister of a big hemlock.
139.A kind heart I better than a crafty head.
140.A small sin is a sister to a big sin.

141. Learning is the stately clothing of the rich man, and the riches of the poor man.
142. The greater the calm, the nearer the South wind.
143. Don't tell me what I was, but tell me what I am.
144. A wise man often makes friend of his enemy.
145. A silent tongue is better than a saying evil.
146. One escape by sheep spoils the whole flock.
147. The death of one dog is the life of another.
148. There is much between saying and doing.

Maori – New Zealand

1. Ask me what is the greatest thing in the world, I will reply: it is the people, it is the people, it is the people, it is the people.
2. Do not boast of your own endeavours.
3. Though my present be small, my love goes with it.
4. Land is permanent, man disappear.
5. It may be small storm yet a successful outcome is imminent.
6. Survival is the treasured goal.
7. There is more than one way to achieve an objective.
8. Let us keep close together, not far apart.
9. Many stars cannot be concealing by a small cloud.
10. Never spent time with people who don't respect you.
11. The more you ask how much longer it will take, the longer the journey seems.
12. The house full of people is a house full of different point of view.
13. He who stands, lives, he who sleeps, dies.
14. The block of wood should not dictate to the carver.
15. Let someone else acknowledge your virtues.
16. A brave who claims trees is food for their roots.
17. The only foolish visit the land of the cannibals.
18. A bird which eats barriers can be caught, but not a bird that eats wood.
19. Turn your face to the sun and the shadows falls behind you.
20. He who yawns catches no fish.
21. Give as well as take and all is well.
22. A large part of strangers attract onlookers.
23. A dog snatches the food and runs.
24. An old man is sick, little hope, if he is young, much.
25. Do not despite a man of small stature.
26. A man of words but not of deeds.
27. Gather the best, reject the bad.

28. Let the industry be rewarded lest idleness get the advantage.
29. A good man is never sought after, a bad looking woman always.
30. Yours is the useful work, mine is ornamental.
31. So evil intentions are hidden as a spider in the web.
32. Good intentions do not last long (then take advantage while they do last).
33. The sun rises to the zenith, the declines.
34. By black of the finger nail....said of narrow escape.
35. A full stomach causes a bird a sing, a man to laugh.
36. A pigeon at home, a noisy parrot on his travels.
37. The priest before, the ordinary folk, after in procession.
38. To keel of a great canoe cannot be lost.
39. A pigeon bolt its food, a parrot eat its bit by bit.
40. Many taro roots an hundred of young dragon ... you cannot destroy them all. That is, you cannot extirpate a tribe.
41. Although it (the gift) is small, it is a gift of love.
42. The goodness of food is brief, you will not gaze upon it long, but a beautiful face will long be gaze upon.
43. It is women and the land that chiefly destroy man.
44. With your food basket and many baskets the people will thrive.
45. Bravery has many resting places.
46. My language, my awakening.
47. Love towards us, love going out from us.
48. Hold fast to the words of your ancestors.
49. Seek the treasure you value most dearly, if you bow your head, let it be to lofty mountain.
50. Although it is small, it is of greenstone.
51. I am a seed scattered from Rangiatea.
52. My bravery is inherited from the chief who were my forbearer.
53. A little adze can do much work as a man.

54. Hold fast to your culture.
55. Care for the land, care for the people, go forward.
56. The pathway of life is often blocked by obstacles, which must be cleared out of the way.
57. Do not lift the paddle out of unison or our canoe will never reach the shore.
58. After little water seeping through a lashing hole may swamp a canoe.
59. Possessions are temporary things compared to the land.
60. Many fail but few succeed
61. The right hand is adept, the left hand is skilful.
62. Think not on the labour, rather reflect on the completion.

Mayans

1. It is not good to throw away your hair, fingernails or teeth because if you don't find them upon your death, you will regret it.
2. It is not good to lie or hide anything from your parents because you don't know what they will change into
3. It is not good to hide good food from visitors because it will turn into worms.
4. It is not good to show laziness on sowing cornfields because the ears of corn will end up twisted.
5. It not good to be lazy when bringing in firewood or you'll fall.
6. It is not good (for pregnant lady) to put a comb in the fold of her skirt because her child's teeth will end up crooked.
7. It is not good to count matches because if there are many that is how many children you will have. (Counting matches is also a waste of time).
8. It is not good for a girl to pass over a boy, because this will be useless.
9. It is not good to hit a dog because it will no longer help you in case you need to pass the flames of fire.
10. It is not good to deny anything to your parents because at the end of our life we will suffer hen tricks.

Morocco

1. The heart of a fool is in his mouth, the mouth of a wise man is in his heart.
2. If a man told you that a dog had run off with your ear, would you go after the dog or search first for your ear?
3. Three things cause sorrow to flee, water, green tree and beautiful face.
4. Plans fail for lack of counsel but with many advisors, succeed.
5. A dog on the run is safely kicked.
6. He who is a mocker dances without tambourine.
7. Some will learn through pain and sorrow, others through joy and laughter, so it is written.
8. To the dog it has money, men say, "my Lord dog".
9. When a dog can bite, it has bone in its mouth.
10. He who touches honey is compelled to lick his fingers.
11. By all means make friends with the dog, but do not lay aside the stick.
12. Better a handful of dried figs and content with that, than to own the gate of peacock and be kicked in the eye by a broody camel.
13. The hand you cannot bite, kiss.
14. He who eats when he is fool digs his grave with his teeth.
15. The driver of an ass must by necessity know its wind.
16. Catch the halter rope and it will lead you to the donkey.
17. With much knowledge there is much sorrow, with much wisdom there is much weeping.
18. Angels bend down their wings to a seeker of knowledge.
19. By all means trust Allah, but tie your camel first.
20. Do not shoot a glass arrow into a painted deer.

21. Open your door to a good day and prepare yourself for bad one.
22. He is a good storyteller who can turn a man's ear into eyes.
23. Pleasant words are honeycomb, sweet to the soul and healing to the bone.
24. An honest answer is like a kiss to the lips.
25. A crucible for silver and a furnace for gold, but Allah test the heart.
26. He who mocks the poor shows contempt for their maker.
27. He who lacks knowledge derides his neighbour, but the man of understanding holds his tongue.
28. If you're going to tell the truth, you better have one foot in the stirrup.
29. A devil takes one and makes two, a saint takes two and makes one.
30. What is past is gone, what is hoped for is absent, for you is the in which you.
31. Few desire, happy life.
32. Better a gurgling of a camel than the prayers of a fish.
33. For he who builds his casbah out of halvah; beware the nibblers.
34. A wise man has much to say and yet remains silent.
35. As the sand of desert is to the weary traveller, so are the words to he who love silent.
36. That which you put into your kettle, comes later into your spoon.
37. If a man puts a cord around his neck, god will provide someone to pull it.
38. A book is like a garden in the pocket.
39. The teacher will appear when the student is ready.
40. For the sake of a single rose, the gardener becomes servant to a thousand thorns.
41. Let us sit bent, but talk straight.
42. Every rose has a thorn as a friend.

43. The camel driver has his plans and the camel has his.
44. If at noon the king declares it is night, behold the stars.
45. If the prayers of the dogs were answered, the bones would rain from the sky.
46. Do not judge a man by whiteness of his turbine, soap is bought on credit.
47. A camel never sees his own hump; those of his brothers are always before him.
48. In his heart a man may plan his course but God determines his every step.
49. The same destiny awaits both the wise man and the fool.
50. Do not correct with a strike, that which can be taught with a kiss.
51. A fool's lips bring him strife and invite a beating.
52. Like a gold ring in a pig snout is a woman without discretion.
53. Better a patient man than a warrior, one who controls his temper than one who takes a city.
54. The mind is a free and the slightest thought has great influence, it is therefore important that you think enlightened thoughts.
55. One pervades the great universe is seen by none unless a man knows the unfolding of love.
56. Man alone is the measure of all things.
57. Every dog thinks of his own fleas as gazelles.
58. He who follows the crow will be led to the corpses of dogs.
59. The dawn does not come twice to awaken a man.
60. The palm of one hand does not eclipse the sun.
61. The best fighting is often against your-self.
62. A narrow space looks wide to the narrow minded.
63. Kindness can pluck the whiskers of a lion.
64. He, who has patience with his enemy, rewards himself.

65. Even a solid rock is unshakable by the wind, so are the wise unshakable by praise or blame.
66. The weight of the burden is known only by he who carries it.
67. If I listen, I have the advantage, if I speak, others have it.
68. The village gate can be closed, the mouth of the fool, never.
69. Without fingers, the hand would be a spoon.
70. Allah gives dried beans to eat to him whom has no teeth left.
71. The barking dog does not hurt the cloud.
72. The tongue has no bone yet it crushes.
73. Often the best way to give oneself what one lacks is take from one self what one has.
74. The understanding of an Arab is in his eyes.
75. Patience is the key to paradise.
76. The candle is put into the lantern, and the moth is left outside, fluttering.
77. The air of heaven is that which blows between the Horse's ears.
78. The bearded of the guest is in the hands of the owner of the tent.
79. If you see him riding on a bamboo cane say to him "Good health to your Horse".
80. Unless you open every door, every door it is fear that hides behind all our movements.
81. Think of the "going out" before you enter.
82. The day has its eyes, the night has ears.
83. The most wonderful thing in the world is success of a fool and the failure of a wise man.
84. A strainer is none the worse for having another hole.
85. Take care. The sleep of nonexistence will overtake you at last, for the coming and going of the breath is but rocking of the cradle.
86. He who houses a camel must make his door higher.

87. A small date stone props up the water jar.
88. May Allah protect me from friends, my enemies I can handle.
89. If the light serves to see, it also serves to be seen.
90. Push a lucky man into the Nile, and he will come up with a fish in his mouth.
91. The moon shines in the absence of the sun – do not strike a rail with your fist, nor mistake the sun for the puff of a candle.
92. Manage with bread and butter until God brings jam.
93. The bear knew nine songs, all were on honey.
94. If you are an anvil, you will suffer like an anvil. If you are hammer, you will strike like a hammer.
95. An egg cannot break a stone.
96. The biggest nuts are those which are empty.
97. Let us sit bent but talk straight.
98. When the chicken's feathers are gold, it isn't smart to make broth out of the hen.
99. The fish in the trap will begin to think.
100. A smooth lie is better than distorted truth.
101. Every Sheep hangs by its own legs.
102. Allah may love poor man, but not a dirty one.
103. Put your dates in the honey pot, but don't sink it afterwards in the mud of Nile.
104. If you make yourself honey, the flies will eat you.
105. To a donkey, on thistle is better than two ass-loads of jewels.
106. When the crow is your guide, he will lead you to the corpses of dogs.
107. Mother a weed, father a weed.
108. One cannot hold two watermelons with one hand.
109. You can count the number of apples in one tree, but you can never count number of trees in one apple.
110. Life is perpetual drunkenness, the pleasure passes, but the headache remains.

111. Life is perpetual drunkenness, it will pleasure passes, but the headache remains.
112. However the eye may rise, it will find the eyebrow above it.
113. If fate throws a knife at you, there are two ways of catching it, by the blade and by the handle.
114. It's easy to carry on war- through a spyglass.
115. When to have put your head into a mortar, it is useless to dread the sound of the pestle.
116. Nourish a vulture and it will pick out your eyes.
117. Whoever pats scorpions with the hand of compassion gets stung.
118. Every knot has an untraveller in Allah.
119. There are many men who are keys to good and locks to evil.
120. O destiny, it pleases you to caress a few- and molest others.
121. The dung heap must make itself smelt before we can breathe the perfume of the flowers.
122. The dogs may bark, but the caravan passes on.
123. A sponge to wipe out the past, a rose to make the present sweet, and a kiss to salute the future.

Native American

1. Listen or your tongue will keep you deaf.
2. Don't judge any man until you have walked two moons in his moccasins.
3. After dark all cats are leopards.
4. Do not wrong your neighbour for it is not he that you wrong but yourself.
5. If you see no reason from giving thanks, the fault lies within yourself.
6. Man has responsibility, not power.
7. Do right and fear no man.
8. Tell me and I will forget, show me and I may remember, involve me and I will understand.
9. Do unto others as you would be done unto you.

Nepal – Nepalese

1. A smart Jackal is not much against an old tiger.
2. Enjoy the heat of a long, and heed the advice of the elders.
3. Parents are like or equal to God.
4. Wealth is both an enemy and a friend.
5. Like cumin in the mouth of an elephant.
6. Opportunity comes but does not linger.
7. It is the mind that wins or loses.
8. One who does not know to dance says the floor is crooked.
9. The monkey's thigh is the shaman's meat.
10. Looking for fire while carrying a lamp.
11. The god's name in the mouth but in the pocket a knife.
12. In the land of mad people, there are insane rituals.

Netherlands Antilles

1. A thorn defends the rose, harmony only those who would steal the blossom.
2. Where the heart loves, there the legs walk.
3. Riches run after the rich, and poverty runs after the poor.

Niger

1. If the owner of the goat is not afraid to travel by night, the owner of a hyena certainly will not be,
2. The cry of a hyena and the loss of the goat are one.
3. Abundance will make cotton pull a stone.
4. Every fault is laid at the door of the hyena, but it does not steal a bale of cloth.
5. Accomplishment of purpose better than making a profit.
6. A proverb is a Horse of conversation: when the conversation lags a proverb receives it.
7. If you watch your pot, your food will not burn.
8. A wise man knows proverbs can reconcile difficulties.
9. Before one cooks, one must have meat.

Nigerian

1. A man does not wander far from where his corn is.
2. A rat is born a rabbit.
3. A tiger does not have to proclaim its tiger attitude.
4. A traveller to distant places should make no enemies.
5. A tree does not move unless there is wind.
6. A tree is best measured when it is down.
7. A tree is known by its fruit.
8. An old man is there to talk.
9. Fine words do not produce food.
10. "Give me a push from my back" does not mean to give me a hunchback.
11. If a monkey is amongst dogs why won't it start barking?
12. If a crocodile eats their own eggs, what would they do to the flesh of the frog?
13. If death be terrible, the fault is not in death, but thee.
14. If one finger brought oil it soiled others.
15. If you fail to take away a strong man's sword when he is on the ground, will you do it when he gets up?
16. It is the fear of offence that makes men swallows poison.
17. It is the first step that is difficult.
18. It takes a village to raise a child.
19. It takes all sorts to make a world.
20. No sane person sharpens his machete to cut a banana tree.
21. No to know is bad, not to wish to know is worse.
22. No to know the good we have, till time has stolen the cherished gift away, is cause of half the misery that we feel, and makes the world the wilderness it is.
23. No to oversee workmen, is to leave your purse open.
24. One goat cannot carry another goat's tail.
25. Profit is profit even in Mecca.
26. The death that will kill a man begins as an appetite.

27. The disobedient foul obeys in the pot of soup.
28. The frog does not jump in the daytime without a reason.
29. The house roof fights the rain but he who is sheltered ignores it.
30. The house sweeper's buttock is never at one direction.
31. The hunter does not rub himself in oil and lie by the fire to sleep.
32. The lizard that jumps from the high iroko tree said he would praise himself is no one else did.
33. The one being carried does not realise how far away town is.
34. When the mice laugh at the cat, there is a whole nearby.
35. When the next house on fire, it's high time to look to your own.
36. You cannot compare the living with the death.
37. You cannot roast corn with two eyes.
38. You cannot run with the hare and hunt with the hounds.
39. A hunter who has only one arrow does not shoot with careless aim.
40. A farmer does not boast that he has had a good harvest until his stock of yams last till the following harvest season.
41. Success is 10% ability and 90% sweet.
42. When a right hand washes the left hand and the left hand washes the right hand, both hands become clean.
43. One does not become a master diviner in a day, a forest is not made a in a season. The swoop of an eagle has seen many seasons and floods.
44. Peter Edoche: it is form a small seed that the giant Iroko tree has its beginning.

45. What an old man sees while lying down, young man can never sees when climbing up in a tree.
46. The child of an elephant will not dwarf.
47. Only the thing which you have struggled will last.
48. Whoever is a patient with a cowries shell will one day have a thousand of them.
49. Seeing is better than hearing.
50. The day o which one starts out is not time to start one's preparations.
51. What a child says, he has heard at home.
52. A wealthy man will always have followers.
53. If you fill your mouth with a razor, you will plight blood.
54. One who has been bitten by the Snake lives in fear of worms.
55. Water may cover the footprint on the ground but it does not cover the words of the mouth.
56. Allah made the silk cotton tree beautiful so let the fig tree cease being angry.
57. He who waits for a chance may wait for long time.
58. However the streams flow, it never forgets its source.
59. Hold a true friend with both hands.
60. Love is like a sea weed, even if you have pushed it away, you will not prevent it from coming.
61. A man who lives alone is either always overworked or always overfed.

Ovambo

1. A parasite cannot live alone.
2. If you do not have patience you cannot make beer.
3. There is not enough room for two elephant to sit in the same shade.

Pakistan

1. The sieve says to the needle; you have a hole in your tail.
2. It is better to turn back than to get lost.
3. All good things come to those who wait.
4. Wise man thinks alike.
5. The best things in life are free.
6. Slow and steady wins the race.
7. Doubt is the beginning of wisdom.
8. Great starts make great finish.
9. What's good for the goose is good for the gander.
10. Epigrams succeed where epic fail.
11. It is nothing for one to know something unless another knows you know it.
12. Go and wake up luck.
13. Do well the little things now, so shall great things come to thee by and by asking to be done.
14. Every man goes down to his death bearing in his hands only that which he has given away.

Palestinian

1. Blood can never turn into water.
2. Hit the iron while it's still hot.
3. The eye can't go any high than the brow.
4. Ask an experienced, and don't ask a philosopher.
5. Keep your white penny for your black day.
6. A bird in the hand is better than ten on the tree.
7. Stay with the measure until he reaches the door.
8. Kiss the dog on his mouth until you get what you need out of him.
9. Stay away from the evil and sing to it.
10. Don't ask the singer to sing until he wishes to sing by himself.
11. Your tongue is your Horse, if you take care of it, it will take care of you, and if you offend it will offend you.
12. Keep your hand tight, you won't bleed and you won't weep.
13. Stretch your legs as long as your quilt can cover.
14. The shoemaker is bare-footed and weaver is naked.
15. The eye can see what the hand cannot reach.
16. The unlucky and hopeless have come together.
17. He who has a flash on his head can keep touching it.
18. A monkey is a deer in his mom's eye.
19. Ground be stronger, none walk on you like myself.
20. The further you are the dearer you become.
21. A dog's tail never straightens out.
22. Every bad bean has its seller.
23. He who takes a monkey for his monkey, the monkey shall go and the monkey shall remain.
24. Behind every mysterious thing is a disaster.
25. A chicken dug in the soil, and the dirt came in her head.
26. He who gets between the onion and its shell shall come out with stinking smell.

27. Look for a needle in a haystack.
28. She who trusts men is one who carries water in a riddle.
29. He's come to sell water in a small water carries.
30. The bald (woman) shows off her niece's hair.
31. Every oppressor has a day.
32. One hand doesn't clap.
33. Truth is comfort.
34. Didn't see them stealing, saw them sorting their shares.
35. We walk by the walls and ask God for shelter.
36. Kissing hand is fooling beard.
37. He couldn't manage the donkey, he managed its saddle.
38. The empty gives the way to the full.
39. Do well and throw it in the sea.
40. Those who dig an evil hole will fall into it.
41. Your close neighbour is better than your far away brother.
42. The house of our fathers and strangers came to kick us out.
43. There will be a day for the oppressor when he will be crushed like garlic.
44. Do not drink from a well and throw a stone into it.
45. Knock on the door before entering.
46. Nobody will plough the land except its Cow.
47. The ignorant it is his own enemy.
48. The one who loves does not hate.
49. Whatever is written on the forehead is always seen.
50. You will not dare mistreating the face you see in the morning.
51. The eye is one that eats.
52. If you feed the mouth, the eye becomes shy.
53. Away from the eye, away from the mind.
54. Do good if you expect to receive it.
55. Do not drink poison to quench a thirst.

56. Every eye has its look.
57. Every Sheep is hung by its own leg.
58. Nobody's perfect.
59. The eye of the master does more work than both his land.
60. Whatever man had done, man may do.

Pasho

1. Learning makes a good man better, an ill man worse.
2. Let each one turn his mind to his own troubles.
3. There is no proverb which is not true.
4. Time soften all grieves.
5. He that respects is respected.
6. He that marries for wealth sells his liberty.
7. Every wrong is avenged on earth.
8. You cannot do anything by doing nothing.
9. Skill is stronger than strength.
10. Deeds not words prove the man.
11. Small mouth, big words.
12. A fly's hostility will be known on the scald-headed man.
13. Say not "I am in the world" God has made man above man.
14. The slave is down, but his vaunting is up.
15. Though I am but a straw, I am as good as you.
16. The frog mounted a cloud, and said it had seen Kashmir.

Persian

1. A bad wound heals but a bad word doesn't.
2. A broken hand works, but not a broken heart.
3. A broken sleeve holdeth them arm back.
4. A stone throw at a right time is better than gold given at a wrong time.
5. A thief is a king till he's caught.
6. A thief he knows a thief as a wolf know a wolf.
7. Be a lion at home and a fox abroad.
8. By a sweet tongue and kindness, you can drag an elephant with a hair.
9. Courteous men learn courtesy from discourteous.
10. Courtesies are cumbersome to them that ken it not.
11. Courtesy on one side can never last long.
12. Do a little things now, so shall big things comes to thee by nad by asking to be done.
13. Do men gather grapes of thorns, figs of thistles?
14. Do well the little things now so shall great things come to thee by and by asking to be done.
15. Epigram succeed where epic fail.
16. Every man goes down to his death bearing in his hands only that which he has given away.
17. Go and wake-up your luck.
18. Go as far as you can see and when you get there you will see further.
19. Go further and fare worse.
20. He gives a party with a bathwater.
21. He gives him a roast meat and beats him with the spit.
22. He who wants rose must respect the thorn.
23. He who wants content can't find an easy chair.
24. I used to feel sorry for myself because I had no shoes until met who was dead.
25. If a man would live in peace, he should be blind, deaf and dumb.

26. If fortune turns against you, even jelly breaks your tooth.
27. If one had to jump a stream and knows how wide it is, he will jump. If he does not know how wide it is, he will jump, and six times out of ten he will make it.
28. If the teacher be corrupt, the world will be corrupt.
29. Luck is infatuated with the efficient.
30. No lamp burns till morning.
31. One pound of learning requires ten pound of common sense to apply it.
32. Taking the first step with the good thought, the second with the good word, and the third with the good deed, I enter paradise.
33. The best memory is that which forgets nothing but injuries. Write kind is marble and write injuries in the dust.
34. The best mode of instruction is to practice what you preach.
35. The best of friends must apart.
36. The blind man is laughing at the bald head.
37. The doctor must heal his own bald head.
38. The loveliest of faces are not to be seen by moonlight, when one sees half with eye and half with the fancy.
39. The wise man sits on the hole in his carpet.
40. Thinking is the essence of wisdom.
41. Use your enemy's hand to catch a snake.
42. Walls have mice and ears.
43. What is brought by the wind will be carried away by the wind.
44. Whatever is in the heart will be come up to the tongue.
45. Whatever you sow, you reap.
46. When the cat and the mouse agree, the grocer is the ruined.
47. What does not beat his own child will later beat his own breast.

48. What does not beat his own child will later beat his own breast.
49. You can't pick up two melons with one hand.
50. You can't please everyone.
51. You can't push on a rope.
52. You can't put new wine in old bottle.
53. You can't squeeze blood from a rock.
54. You can't take blood from a stone.
55. A drowning man is not troubled by rain.
56. An egg thief becomes a camel thief.
57. He who has been bitten by a snake fears a piece of string.
58. In the ant's house the dew is a flood.
59. Injustice all around is justice.
60. Stretch your foot to the length of your blanket.
61. The larger a women roof the more snow it collects.
62. Do not cut down the tree that gives you shade.

Portuguese

1. A bad knife cuts one's finger instead of the stick.
2. A barking dog was never a good hunter.
3. A barley corn is better than a diamond to a rock.
4. A beard lathered is halved shaved.
5. A beard once washed is half shaven.
6. A beggar's wallet is never full.
7. A busting mother makes a slothful daughter.
8. A contented ass enjoys a long life.
9. Dogs in the manager that neither eats nor let others eat.
10. A dead man does not speak.
11. A dull is near home trots without the stick.
12. A fast horse does not want the spur.
13. A fault confessed is half redressed.
14. A finger's length in a sword and a palm in a lance are a great advantage.
15. A finger's length in a sword, and a palm in a lance, is a great advantage.
16. A friend is to be taken without his faults.
17. A friend's fault is to be known but not abhorred.
18. A full man is no eater.
19. A girl, a vineyard, an orchard, and a bean field, are hard to watch.
20. A good cock was never fat.
21. A good thing is known when it is lost.
22. A good thing is soon caught up.
23. A good word quenches more than a cauldron of water.
24. A good year is determined by its spring.
25. A goose cannot graze after him.
26. A goose, a woman, and a goat are bad thing to lean.
27. A gossiping woman talks of everybody, and everybody of her.
28. A great thrust of a lance at a dead Moor.

29. A house without either a cat or a dog is a house of a scoundrel.
30. A hungry belly hears nobody.
31. A hungry wolf is not at rest.
32. A little gall spoils much money.
33. A little injury dismays, and a great one stills.
34. A little knowledge is a dangerous thing.
35. A little leak will sink a great ship.
36. A man of straw is better than a woman of gold.
37. A little makes a debtor and much an enemy.
38. A morsel eaten gains no friend.
39. A pig on credit makes a good winter and a bad spring.
40. A poor man is hungry after eating.
41. A rugged colt may make a handsome Horse.
42. A rash man, a skin of good wine, and a glass vessel, do not last long.
43. A resolute heart endures no counsel.
44. A rich widow weeps with one eye and signal with another.
45. A seat in the council is honour without profit.
46. A servant and a cock must be kept but one year.
47. A shut mouth keeps me out of strife.
48. A small hatchet fells a great oak.
49. A small peck becomes a small peddler.

Russian

1. A field held in common is always ravaged by bears.
2. A jug that has been mended last two hundred years.
3. A Lizard on a cushion will still seek leaves.
4. An enemy will agree, but a friend will argue.
5. An icy may fills granaries.
6. An indispensable thing never has much value.
7. An old loan repaid is like finding something new.
8. As long as the child does not cry it does not matter what pleases it.
9. Bad luck is fertile.
10. Devils live in quite bond.
11. Don't worry if you borrow, but worry if you lend.
12. Even a coffin is made to measure.
13. Everyday learns from the other that went before, but no day teaches the one that follows.
14. God wanted to chastised mankind, so he sent lawyers.
15. Golden hands, but wicked mouth.
16. Happiness is not a Horse, you cannot harness it.
17. He that has no heart, let him have heels.
18. He that is afraid of bad luck will never know good.
19. If you put your noise into water, you will also wet your cheeks.
20. In the kingdom of hope there is no winter.
21. It is easy to undress the naked.
22. It is good to sleep in whole skin.
23. Many who have gold in the house are looking for copper outside.
24. No matter how much you feed the Wolf he will always return to the forest.
25. No one is dragged to heaven by the hair.
26. One son is no son, two sons is no son, but three sons is a son.
27. Only a fool will make the doctors his heir.

28. Sit a beggar at your table and he will soon put his feet on it.
29. Small children give you headache, big children heartache.
30. Some people are masters of money, and some it's slaves.
31. Take thy thoughts to bed with thee, for the morning is wiser than evening.
32. The coal is quite new, only the holes are old.
33. The horses of hope gallop, but the asses of experience go slowly.
34. The lucky man's enemy dies and unlucky man's friend.
35. The older bear falls into old trap.
36. There is plenty of sound in an empty barrel.
37. They bow to you when borrowing; you bow to them when collecting.
38. They gave a naked man a shirt and he said it was too thick.
39. To run away is not glorious but very healthy.
40. What the rake gathers, the fork scatters.
41. When rubbles fall from heaven there is no sack, when there is a sack rubbles don't fall.
42. When we sing everybody hears us, when we sigh nobody hears us.
43. Wild duck and tomorrow both come without calling.
44. With seven nurses the child lose it eye.

Rwanda

1. In court of fowls, the cockroach never wins his case.
2. In a fiddler's house all are dreams.
3. You can outdistance that which is running after you, but not what is running inside you.
4. You can take the boy out of the country but you can't take the country out of the boy.
5. The real voyage of discovery consist not seeing new landscape but in having new eyes.
6. A rapid stream wears itself out.

Sanskrit

1. The anger of virtuous men is pacified easily but the wicked never give up their grievances. After all, gold can be melted, but who can melt mere grass.
2. Just as a chameleon changes colours, the low and the wicked too put on the different colours, at first, he acts as a relative, next as a friend and at the end, he turns out to be and enemy.
3. Even when honoured, rogues do not forget their wickedness. Does a crescent become round even after residing on the head of Lord Shiva.
4. The character of a wise man that has knowledge and wisdom in the right measure is this- he does not become despondent in adversity, and does not become arrogant in times of prosperity.
5. Virtuous conduct, cleanliness, courtesy, sweet disposition and noble birth... all these do not shine in a person who does not possess wealth.
6. Honour, self respect, knowledge, bravery, high deals... all these are fruitless if one does not have wealth.
7. A woman 's appetite is twice that of a man's her sexual desire four times, her intelligence, eight times.
8. All we can hold in our cold dead hands is what we have given.
9. He who allows his day without practising and enjoying life's pleasure is like a blacksmith's bellows; he breathes but does not live.
10. If you forsake certainty and depend on an uncertainty, you will lose both the certainty and uncertainty.
11. If you gentle touch a nettle it will sting you for your pains, grasp it like a lad of mettle, and as soft as silk remain.
12. Sorrow for the death of a father lasts six months, sorrow for a mother, a year, sorrow for a wife, until another wife, sorrow for a son, forever.

13. Yesterday is but a dream; tomorrow is but a vision, but today well lived makes yesterday a dream of happiness, and every tomorrow a vision of hope, look well, therefore, to this day.
14. Break the pots. Tear the clothes. Ride a donkey, by whatever means possible, a man should become famous.
15. Where woman are worshiped, goddess's dwell. Where woman they are not worshiped, all actions are fruitless.
16. A fool is worshiped at home.
17. A chief is worshiped in his own town.
18. A king is worshiped in his own kingdom.
19. A knowledgeable person is worshiped everywhere.
20. Of a person who has money and a little intellect, all his action gets destroyed.
21. One should not regret the past; one should not worry about the future. Wise men act by the present time.
22. Even when instigated by others, the mind of a pious person never hesitates (to take the right decision). In is not possible to heat the water of the ocean by torch of dried grass.
23. Look well to this day, for it is life, the very life of life, the very life of life. In it lie all realities and verities of existence, of bliss of growth, the glory of action, splendour of beauty. For yesterday is but a dream, and tomorrow only a version of hope. Look well, therefore, to this day, for it and alone, is life? Such is the salutation of dawn.
24. A creeper that has been cut can be made to grow again, but it never looks as beautiful as it use to. Similarly, an affectionate relationship that has been spoilt can be revived again, but it will not have the same charm as it used.
25. A noble man makes a gift of charity respectfully and without publicity. Mean men also practice charity, but

they are guided by selfish motive and give away with disrespect.

26. Friendship with the good grows day by day just as the sap of from the top to bottom, joint by joint.
Friendship of the wicked is opposite in nature to this.

27. Foolish people never give up enmity, just as a line drawn on a rock cannot be erased. But the wise forgive and forget, their enmity is as ephemeral as line drawn on the surface of water.

28. Where fools pretend to be wise, the wise should pretend to be foolish, under the spell of ignorance ridicule even the wise saying.

29. Avoid even the sight of foolish me, if one does not see them, then avoid the company, if one does not fall into the company of foolish men, then let him keep silence. And if one does not have to speak amongst them, and then let him to speak like them.

30. If one is censured for a genuine fault of his, then he should endure that rebuke. And if he is censured for no fault of his, he should the others person thinking that the censure did not occur at all.

31. If a dog bites a man, he does not bite the dog back. Therefore, if a wicked man humiliates a virtuous one, the letter should not seek revenge.

32. Following are characteristics of a bad friend- making fun of their friend in public, showing friendship only as some benefit is obtained from the friendship, and not forgetting the bad deeds of his friend towards him.

33. One should retain formal courtesy as long as friendship has not been achieved. Once friendship is acquired, formal courtesy is a sign of deceit.

34. Just as a female bee gathers so much honey little by little that I can fill several pots. Likewise, wise man gathers knowledge, religious merit and penance little by little continuously without ever giving up.

35. Even old man should humbly approach younger men with reverence and clarification on their doubts, just as they would approach their teachers with respect.
36. One should strive to become learned and not hanker after wealth alone, it is common to find a wealthy man, but rare indeed is he who has erudition.
37. Of what use is a long life to those whose minds are blemished with lust and jealous, who work inefficiently and who feel insulted at slight pretext.
38. Although dim, the rays of the moon falling on the snow clad peaks of the Himalayas look resplendent and illuminate entire mountain range. Like-wise even a few good qualities become abundant in person who are lofty with merit.
39. The wealth of a man who merely hoards riches, but does not want to enjoy them is like someone else's wealth lying in his house. It is like a daughter brought up (with love and affection) only to be given away at the time of marriage.
40. No purpose of existence and no object of human life is attained by him, who turn misery at the sight of a needy man and turn him away.
41. That man's life long is meaningful who sustains and nourishes vast multitude of men from his provisions, and he who does not sustain his dependents is indeed dead, even if alive.
42. A wise man should not speak ill of others in an assembly. Even that truth should not be uttered which, if expressed becomes unpalatable.
43. Why should man endowed with good sense speak harshly, when sweetness is with their own power and when sentences can be composed with sweet words?
44. When a person is addressed harshly, he responds in a doubly harsh manner. There, one who does not wish to hear unpleasant words must not use such a language.

45. He is an eloquent speaker who speaks with brevity but whose speech is sweet. One who speaks a lot but speaks with little sense is nothing but a prattler.
46. As a fire is extinguished only by water, similarly, the anger caused by harsh speech can be pacified only by the words of wisdom spoken by virtuous.
47. Learning, verdict study, penances, prosperity, fame and splendour are all these in one who is devoid of good character are like the bath of an elephant (an elephant through dust on his body after bathing).
48. Pilgrimage to holy place for ablutions, gazing at the hot blazing, such as penance, standing in water in winter all these cannot take a man to heaven if he were devoid of good character.
49. Of what use are garlands and perfumes to the man, the fragrance of whose noble qualities has permeated all direction.
50. The following virtues are inborn and natural in nobles persons, appreciation of merit of others concealing one's own merits and not publicize them for fame, not criticizing the faults of men in front of others, to defame them, sweet disposition and straightforward speech.
51. An ignoble man, though born of a noble lineage, endowed with eloquence and adorned with garlands is like the Palasa (flame of forest) tree which blooms but does not yield any fruit.
52. A wicked man feels elated when he hurts others with his unkind words. On the contrary, a good man repents immediately even if he makes unkind remarks out of carelessness.
53. A small good done to the virtuous bears great results, while even great help extended to the wicked begets only sorrow. Behold even grass fed to cows turns into milk, where areas if milk is fed to Snakes, it becomes a deadly poison.

54. Even at times of calamity, a noble man should desist from harbouring ill-will or enmity towards others. He is like the sandalwood tree that imparts its fragrance even to the axe blade that strikes it down.

Scanian

1. Out of all cookery, the coffee laced with schnapps is the best.
2. It's too late to rise early when you wake up at eleven o'clock.
3. She would be a nice girl if she didn't have her head.
4. The medicine that cures the tailor can kill a shoe maker.
5. Dead men are hard to wake.
6. Eat and take belly, because tomorrow the assistant of the executioner will come to take the skin.
7. You shouldn't eat valium before going out.
8. After the meal, one had to be still and shut the eyes for a while in the gloom.
9. Tasty goose is too small for two but too big for one.
10. A Scanian is only Swedish during ice hockey world championship.
11. I'll come again said the woman who got caught in wing of windmill.
12. The food is half the provision, the rest is herring and potatoes.
13. The mare of the smith and the children of the shoemaker always go barefooted.
14. A youngster can ask further than an aged has been.

Scottish

1. Better bend than breaks.
2. A man is lion in his own cause.
3. A tale never loses in the telling.
4. Be happy while you are living, for you are a long time dead.
5. Be slow in choosing a friend, but slower in changing him.
6. Better be ill spoken of by one before all than by all before one confessed faults are half mended.
7. Open confession is good for the soul.
8. Don't marry for money, you can borrow it cheaper.
9. Egotism is an alphabet of one letter.
10. Either a man or a mouse.
11. Fools look for tomorrow, wise man use tonight.
12. Get what you can and keep what you have, that's the way to get rich.
13. Learn young, learn fair, learn old, and learn more.
14. Luck never gives, it only lends.
15. Never draw your dirk when a blow will do it.
16. Never let your feet run faster than your shoes.
17. Take care of your pennies and your dollars will take care of themselves.
18. The day has eyes, the night has ears.
19. The devil's boots don't creak.
20. There never came ill of good advertisement.
21. They are good that are away.
22. They talk of my drinking but never my thirst.
23. They that dance must pay the fiddler.
24. They that live longest, see most.
25. They that smell least smell best.
26. They that sow the wind shall reap the whirlwind.
27. They that will not be counselled cannot be helped.
28. Twelve highlanders and a bagpipe make a rebellion.

29. What may be done at anytime will be done at no time.
30. When the cup is full, carry it even.
31. Wilful waste makes woeful want.
32. A begun turn is half ended.
33. A blate cat makes a proud mouse.
34. A black hen lays a white egg.
35. A blithe heart makes a blooming look.
36. Abundance of law breaks none.
37. A hungry stomach is eye craving.
38. A cock's eye cruse on his ain't midden-head.
39. A dry simmer never made a deer peck.
40. A hungry louse bite sair.
41. A light purse makes a heavy heart.
42. A penny saved is a penny gained.
43. Cutting out well is better than sewing up well.
44. He that loves law will get his fill of it.
45. It is ill fishing if the hook is bare.
46. It is sin and not poverty that makes man miserable.
47. Money is flat and was meant to be plied up.
48. Never go to the devil and dish-clout is your hand.
49. One may ride a free horse to death.
50. The first dish pleaseth all.
51. To marry is to half your rights and double your duties.
52. What bites one, banes another.
53. When all fruits fail, welcome haws.
54. What's for you will not go by you.
55. A child may have too much of his mother's blessing.
56. A cold need the cook as much as the doctor.
57. Bees that have honey in their mouths have sting in their tails.
58. a dry lent, a fertile year.
59. Better keep the devil at the door than turn him out of the house.
60. When then heart is full the tongue will speak
61. It is better to try than to hope.

62. Every flood will have ebb.
63. Long sleep makes hot rowing.
64. One cow breaks the fence, and a dozen leap it.
65. Better to hear the evil than see it.
66. I would know your gifts by your graciousness.
67. Where the stream is shallowest, great is its noise.
68. Every straw is a thorn at night.
69. It's a long river whose head can't be found.
70. Through separation be hard, two never met but had to part.
71. The best of nursing may overcome the worse disease.
72. All the keys to the land do not hang from girdle.
73. If bad the raven, his company is no better.
74. It is easy to keep a castle that's not besieged.

Serbia

1. A foolish fox is caught by one leg, but a wise one by all four.
2. It is easier to believe than to go and ask.
3. A greedy father has thieves for children.
4. The best inheritance a parent can give to his children is few minutes of their time each day.
5. Children learn to smile from their parent.
6. If you want your children to improve, let them overhear the nice things you say about them to others.
7. Any angry father is most cruel towards himself.
8. A greedy man God hates.
9. A thorn pierces the skin more quickly than old.
10. Good deeds are the best prayers.
11. The glory of ancestors should not prevent a man winning.
12. A good reputation is better than a golden girdle.
13. A clean pig makes lean bacon.
14. A dead man pays no debt.
15. A man without enemies is worthless.
16. A wife is frightened of her first husband and a husband is frightened of his second wife.
17. After a trial one party is naked and the other without a shirt.
18. An empty knapsack is heavier to carry than full one.
19. Be humble for you are made of dung; be noble for you are made of stars.
20. A tree near the road is easily cut down.
21. Better retreat in honour than advance in disgrace.
22. Do not measure the Wolf's tail till he is dead.
23. Even the devil knows what is right but he will not do it.
24. Everyone is worth more than his neighbour and less than his son.
25. He, who drinks on credit, gets drunk twice.

26. If you can't hold on to the horse's mane, then don't try to hand on to its tail.
27. It does not harm now and then to burn a candle for the devil.
28. It is better to be threatening by the sword of a Turk than by a pen of German.
29. It is better to make money in the straw market than to lose it in money market.
30. It is difficult to find a man but it is easy to recognise him.
31. It is easy to advice the wise.
32. It is easy to tempt a frog to the river.
33. It is not at the table but in prison that you learn who your true friends are.
34. Jealous and fear have big eyes.
35. Let war be waged in the house of him who wants it.
36. Money and the devil know no rest.
37. Mother earth promised to tell her secrets to heaven.
38. One devil does not scratch out another devil's eye.
39. Peace pays what war wins.
40. Quick to believe is quickly deceived.
41. Solitude is full of God.
42. The first marriage is plate of honey, the second a glass of wine, and the third a cup of prison.
43. The wound heals the scars remains.
44. There is nothing worse than a person looking for quarrel.
45. Time builds castles, and time destroys them.
46. To believe is easier than investigation.
47. To serve our elders is a duty, our equals it is polite, but serving the young is humiliating.
48. To set fire to a church is not so bad as to speak ill of a virgin.
49. We won the war, but lost the peace.
50. What is it to be a gentleman? Firstly it is to be thankful and secondly to complain.

51. What is the use of a big wide world when your shoes are too small?
52. What makes you tired makes you stronger.
53. When a stepmother moves in, the father becomes a stepfather.
54. When big bell rings, little ones are not heard.
55. When coins rattle, philosophers are silent.
56. When your wine is finished, conversation ends, when your money has been spent, you lose your friend.
57. Where there are no dogs the wolves will howl.
58. You can judge what you make by what others make.
59. You don't need a candle to look for a fool.
60. You never get headache from winning.

Somalian

1. He, who does not seize opportunity, will be unable to seize tomorrow's opportunity.
2. A camel can tolerate a heavy load, but not crooked rope.
3. A man throws stones not words.
4. Ever camel was once upon a time two years old.
5. You don't go searching for bones in a Lion's den.
6. A coward dies before the courageous dies.
7. An escaped lies does not reach the truth.
8. You lend a false ear to false words.
9. Married couples are neither enemies nor friends.
10. A man one year elder to you is one cunning year elder to you.
11. One should rise to a person who sees you sitting.
12. A deer is an elder to its family.
13. Let what is on this side of the bank be washed out by the flood, what is on that side of the bank be carried away by the wind.
14. A madman does not lack wisdom.
15. You should discuss over a dog's hide when it concerns your interest.
16. Dogs understand each other by their barking and men by their words.
17. The ear cannot hold a much water as it does news.
18. A dog which refuses a bone is not alive.
19. A brave man dies once, a coward a thousand times.
20. One shares food not words.
21. When a man sleeps, it is the same person when he wakes up.
22. The most dangerous thing a man needs is a woman.
23. The child you sired hasn't sired you.
24. There is always a better man for every good man.
25. A man who has eaten something becomes shy.
26. These youth taught their mothers to give birth.

27. One refusing a sibling's advice breaks his arm.
28. A cat in her house has the teeth of a lion.
29. One doesn't tell a man "go away" but one shows him something so he will.
30. A man prolonging his age sees a camel giving birth.
31. Your woman should be in the house or in the grave.
32. A thousand assassinations, one marriage.
33. Men for tea, women for talk.
34. To be without knowledge is to be without light.
35. An old wound will not go away.
36. Do not walk into a snake pit with your eyes open.
37. Wisdom does not come overnight.
38. In the ocean, one does not need to sow water.
39. Where I make my living, there is my home.
40. He who does not shave you does not cut you.
41. The bridge is repaired only after someone fall in the water.
42. To try and fail is not laziness.
43. Poverty is slavery.
44. Think before you do.
45. Sorrow is like rice in the store, if a basketful is removed every day, it will come to an end at last.

Spanish

1. A blustering night, a fair day follows.
2. A dog does not always bark at the front gate.
3. A friend to everybody and nobody is the same thing.
4. A good grievance is better than bad payment.
5. A good man's pedigree is little hunted up.
6. A handsome man is not quite poor.
7. A horseshoe that clatters wants a nail.
8. A man who prides himself on his ancestry is like the potato plant, the best part of which is underground.
9. A mistress in high place is not a bad thing.
10. A rose too often smelled loses its fragrance.
11. An ounce of blood is worth more than a pound of friendship.
12. Beads about the neck, and the devil in the heart.
13. Better a quite death than a public misfortune.
14. Between brothers, two witnesses and notary.
15. Between two Saturdays happen many marvels.
16. Business today, tomorrow never.
17. Choose a wife on Saturday rather than on Sunday.
18. Cow of many, well milked and badly fed.
19. Do not rejoice at my grief, for when mine is old, yours will be new.
20. Even a seek man shuns death.
21. Every cask smells of the wine it contained.
22. Every season brings its own joy.
23. Every woman has something of a witch about her.
24. Experience is not always the kindest of teacher, but it is surely the best.
25. God comes to see without ringing the bell.
26. God gives almonds to those who have no teeth.
27. Growing old is more than another bad habit.
28. Half is twelve miles when you have fourteen miles to go.

29. Happy is the doctor who is called in at the decline of an illness.
30. He that doth not rob makes not a rob or argument.
31. He that has a good harvest must be content with a few thistles.
32. He that is rich will not called a fool.
33. He that marries a widow will often have a dead man's head thrown into dish.
34. He who is contented is not always rich.
35. He, who knows nothing, doubts nothing.
36. I dance to the tune that is played.
37. If the sky falls, hold up your hands.
38. If you pay not a servant his wages he will pay himself.
39. If you want a fine wife, don't pick her on a Sunday.
40. If you want a good service, serve yourself.
41. If you would live in health, be old early.
42. In a calm sea every man is a pilot.
43. In the street of by- and – by one arrives at the house of "never".
44. It is better to be born a beggar than a fool.
45. It is better to conceal one's knowledge than to reveal one's ignorance.
46. It is better to weep with wise men than laugh with fools.
47. It is good to have friends even in hell.
48. Knowledge, teaching and words may be deeds.
49. Let your heart guide your head in evil matter.
50. Love is like war, begins when you like and leave off when you can.
51. Love, pain and money cannot be kept secret, they soon betray themselves.
52. Never marry a widow unless her first husband was hanged.
53. Never offer your hen for sale on a rainy day.
54. No man is quick enough to enjoy life to the full.
55. One lawyer will make work for another.

56. Poverty is not perversity.
57. Punishment is a cripple, but it arrives.
58. Raise ravens and they will peck your eyes.
59. Stars are not seen by sunshine.
60. Sunday's wooing draws to rain.
61. Take head of an ox before, as an ass behind, and a monk on all sides.
62. The best mirror is an old friend.
63. The devil is seldom out shot in his own bow.
64. The fear of a woman is the basis of good health.
65. The man who does not love a horse cannot love a woman.
66. The only chaste woman is the one who has not been chased.
67. The stolen ox sometimes puts his head out of the stall.
68. The wolf loses his teeth, but not his inclinations.
69. The world is a round gulf, and he who cannot swim must go to the bottom.
70. There is no better surgeon than one with many sears.
71. To deny all, is to confess all.
72. To whom you tell your secrets, to him you resign your liberty.
73. Tomorrow is often the busiest day of the week.
74. Tomorrow is often the busiest time of the year.
75. Truth and oil always come to the surface.
76. Visit your aunt, not every day of the year.
77. We make more enemies by what we say than friends by what we do.
78. What belongs to everybody belongs to nobody.
79. When fortunes knocks upon the door open it widely.
80. Where there is no love there is no pain.
81. Who knows most speaks least.
82. Who ties well, unties well.

Swahili

1. The torture of the grave is only known by the corpse.
2. A reserved will not decay.
3. He who praises rain has been rained on.
4. Great wit drives away wisdom.
5. He who does not admit defeat is not a sportsman.
6. He wanders around by day by a lot, learns a lot.
7. If you are absent you lose share.
8. After hardship comes relief.
9. An evil Indian but his business is good.
10. A flag follows the direction of the wind.
11. The evil spirit of a man is a man.
12. The drunkard's money is being consumed by palm-wine dapper.
13. A handsome finger gets the ring.
14. A sinking vessel needs no navigation.
15. Constant dipping will empty gourd of honey.
16. Blood is thicker than water.
17. The remedy of fire is fire.
18. The curse of the fowl does not bother the kite.
19. Gratitude of a donkey is a kick.
20. A weapon which you don't have in a hand won't kill a snake.
21. Follow bees and you will get honey.
22. Put a riddle to a fool a clever person will solve it.
23. The skin of yesterday's sugarcane is a harvest of an ant.
24. Little by little fills up the measure.
25. There is no distance that has no end.
26. There is no secret between two people.
27. Hurry, hurry, has no blessing
28. Anger brings loss(damage)
29. It is better to lose your eye than to lose you is a harvest of an ant.
30. Better to stumble with toe than tongue.

31. Voluntary is better than force.
32. He laughs at the sear who has received no wound.
33. Kindness does not go rotten.
34. If you don't know deaths look at the grave.
35. A good name shines in the dark.
36. An ivory tooth is not cure for the lost tooth.
37. Effort will not counter faith.
38. The village cock does not crow in town.
39. A infidel who does you good turns is not like a Muslim who does not.
40. A rope parts where it is thinnest.
41. A genuine fowl not lay eggs on strange places.
42. A bad job is not worthless as a good name.
43. The creaking of the door deprives me of no sleep.
44. Nine is near ten.
45. Arrogance is not gentlemanly.
46. Everyone should contribute when collection is made.
47. One finger cannot kill a louse.
48. That is fashionable in town is never prohibited.
49. The witch eats you up is in your clothing.
50. Every vessel has its own key.
51. Every door with its own key.
52. To every child his own neck ornaments.
53. Everyone who stretches a skin on a drum pulls the skin on his own side.
54. Every bird flies with its own wings.
55. The bereaved begins the wailing later others join.
56. Along silence followed by mighty noise.
57. One fire brand after another keeps fire burning.
58. A barber does not shave himself.
59. Mouth is the home of words.
60. What the heart desires is medicine to it.
61. A new thing is a source of joy even if is sore.
62. What is not eaten by man let the devil eat it.
63. You cannot know the bugs of a bed that you have lain on.

64. Shadow of a stick cannot protect one from the sun.
65. A good thing sells itself a bad one advertises itself.
66. A handful of water cannot be grasped.
67. One fault does not warrant divorce of a wife.
68. A goshawk is an egg child, if sleeps hungry it's his own fault.
69. One eye of a master sees more than four of a servant.
70. Giving advice but no one listen.
71. The fear of God is not wearing a white turban.
72. Leave well alone. You won't improve matters by going on tinkering.
73. Death has its advantage too, i.e. it benefits those who inherit.
74. Death of not a relative is a wedding compared to a death of a relative.
75. When the head of the family dies, the family breaks up.
76. To live long is too see much.
77. To stumble is not falling down but is to go forward.
78. Borrowing is like a wedding, repaying is like mourning.
79. A Hen does not break her own eggs.
80. A new fowl always strings around its legs.
81. Eating is sweet, digging is weariness.
82. It is not hard to nurse a pregnancy, but it is hard to bring up a child.
83. Where there is mourning someone has died.
84. The timid crow withdraws its wings from harm.
85. You may climb a thorn tree, and be unable to come down.
86. To get lost is to learn the way.
87. Charity is the matter of the heart not of the pocket.
88. Old rust is for the stranger.
89. Cooling the tong is not the end of forging.
90. Timidity often ends in a laugh, bravado in a lament.
91. To run is no necessarily to arrive.
92. Where there are trees, there are no builders.

93. A vessel running aground has no captain.
94. There is no incense for something rotting.
95. One's foul smelling does not sicken oneself but merely disgust one.
96. Today is today who says tomorrow is liar.
97. That which is written by God is what is.
98. Thing don't just happen by accidents.
99. What is being talked about here, and it's not its coming around behind.
100. Out of sight out of mind.
101. Don't take vengeance on silliness.
102. Eyes have no screens; they see all that is within view.
103. Two Bulls do not live in the same shade.
104. A dead person is not asked for a shroud.
105. Water follows current i.e. swim with current.
106. Water flows down the valley does not climb the hill.
107. If you take off your clothes for water you must bath.
108. You cannot know the extent of water in a pond that you never been to.
109. When tide is high, it ebbs.
110. He who climbs a ladder comes down again.
111. If water is split, it cannot be gathered up.
112. Big house conceal a lot.
113. Regrets are like a child, they come some considerable time after event.
114. With any captains, the ship does not sail.
115. Words alone won't break bones.
116. Pleasant words will draw the snake from its hole.
117. When a poor man gets something he boasts of his new wealth.
118. A poor man with his child a rich man with his wealth.
119. Why drive away fowls from the dung you do not eat yourself.
120. Old dropping do not stink.
121. A poor man does not pick up things if they say he stole them.

122. Running on the roof finishes at the edge.
123. One who selects his hoe is not a real farmer.
124. He who select a coconut with great care ends up getting bad coconut
125. You don't throw stones at an approaching crackling noise in the bush wait and see what it is first.
126. A traveller does not make a mess where he had made a camp as he might one day come back.
127. He, who fears crying of a child, will cry himself.
128. Rice is all one but there are many ways of cooking it.
129. He who laughs at a cripple will not dies without becoming himself.
130. A dance will not become a cripple for dancing calls for grace.
131. He who dances at home will be rewarded.
132. He who plays with mud will get splashed.
133. He who ridicules the good will be overtaken by evil.
134. He who digs a pit will fall into it himself.
135. The maker of a wooden spoon saves his hand from fire.
136. He who dips his finger into honey does not dip it once.
137. He, who earns calamity, eats with his family.
138. He, who earns his living in the sun, eats in the shade.
139. He who ridicules a deformed person becomes deformed himself.
140. The teeth of a dog do not lock together. (brothers don't harm each other)
141. One who hides private parts won't get a child.
142. A potter eats from potsherd.
143. One who follows bees will never fail to get honey.
144. One who is expelled from home has nowhere to go.
145. A lazy person with a nephew does not eat dry rice.
146. A witch doctor does not cure himself.
147. Let the guest come so that the host may benefit.
148. I am a mud hut, I cannot stand shock.
149. A sick person is not asked for porridge.

150. When a fool becomes enlightened, the wise man is in trouble.
151. A messenger is not killed.
152. The one who is caught with the skin is the thief.
153. He who fixes his mind much on water ends up not drinking it.
154. A poor man has no contempt.
155. A wife is like clothes and banana plant needs wedding..
156. A single hand cannot slaughter a Cow.
157. A single hand cannot nurse a child.
158. An empty hand is not licked.
159. Kiss the hand you cannot cut.
160. It's nice to throw a spear to a pig, but painful when thrown to you.
161. The farmer is one but those who eat fruits of his labour are many.
162. He who eats another man's food will have his own food eaten by others.
163. He who eats bitter things gets sweet things too.
164. He who devours his neighbour's fowl, its footprint will give him away.
165. The eater of a goat pays back a cow.
166. He who eats with you will not die with you except he who was born with you.
167. He who enjoys the first fruit of a country is the son of that country.
168. One, who keeps silent, endures.
169. He who drinks water with one hand finds out his thirst is still here.
170. Take one, not that you may return with ten.
171. Fire does not begets fire in the end it begets ashes.
172. One who rides two Horses at once will split asunder.
173. He who sows disorderly fashion will eat likewise.
174. He who fights with a wall will only hurt his hand.

175. He who becomes blind in his old ages does not lose his way.
176. A traveller is poor, even though he being a ruler.
177. A hunter is not afraid of thorns.
178. One who talks to himself cannot be wrong, i.e. no one to correct him.
179. If an arrow goes into the forest it is not lost.
180. A tailor does not select his cloth.
181. Do not abuse midwives while child-bearing continues.
182. Patient man will eat ripe fruits.
183. He who requires what is under the bed must bend for it.
184. He who boasts of his ancestry unduly will bring plenty of trouble upon him.
185. He who desires to make something does not announce his intention, just turn them into action.
186. He, who desires all, misses all.
187. He who likes to eat cows hump will not fail to grow fat.
188. An aimless wonder wears away his legs.
189. A connoisseur never comes to the end of desire.
190. A log cannot move save by the help of rollers.
191. An old man always keeps something in reserve.
192. When a child cries out for a razor gives it to him .i.e. let him learn by experience.
193. As you bring up a child, so he will be.
194. The child of a snake is a snake.
195. A person scratches himself where his hand can reach.
196. A person does not object to being called what he is called for.
197. A person is asked about his dress not what he has eaten.
198. One who always depends on his brother will die poor.
199. The carrier of a secret message is not told its meaning.
200. Serve even unbeliever to attain your own ends.

201. A husband of a mother is a father.
202. God does not cancel a liar.
203. One who stores half grown fruits eats it rotten.
204. Abuses are the result of seeing one another too often.
205. Aiming isn't hitting.
206. Haste does not result in prosperity.
207. Haste is from devil.
208. Haste makes waste and waste makes want.
209. The hyena eats the sick man, he will eat whole one.

Syrian

1. If your friend is honey, don't lick him all.
2. The camel limped from its split lip.
3. Chose the neighbour before the house.
4. My brother and I against my cousin, my cousin and I against a stranger.
5. What is past is dead.
6. The rope of a lie is short.
7. Haste is the devil's work and patience is from God the merciful.
8. The son of duck is a floater.
9. We taught them how to beg, they raced us to the gates.
10. A beggar and he bargains.
11. In the eye of his mother, a Monkey is a gazelle.
12. With the lack of Horses, we saddle the Dogs.
13. The eloquent cock crowns from the egg.
14. Patience is the key to relief.
15. He hit me and cried, he raced me to complain.
16. Stretch your legs according to your quilt.
17. A bird at hand is better than ten on the tree.
18. Ask one who has experience rather than a physician.
19. He is like a deaf man at wedding procession.
20. It is not every time that the clay pot survives.
21. He who has his hand in the water is not like him who has his hand in the free.
22. God send almonds to those without teeth.
23. A better one in another one.
24. Every knot has someone to undo it.
25. Keep away from trouble and sing to it.
26. As you went, so you came back.
27. Spend what is in your pocket, you will get more from the unknown.
28. Let the water melon break each other.

29. He married the monkey for its money, the money went and the monkey stayed a monkey.
30. Whoever gets between the onion and its will get nothing but its stink.
31. If you buy cheap meat you will be sorry when you come to the gravy.
32. When the lions are away, the hyenas play.
33. Turn the pots upside down; the girl will still be like mother.
34. When we decide to trace coffins, people decide not to die.
35. Let your money be insulted but not yourself.
36. Having faith in men is like faith that water will remain in a sieve.
37. Let it wound your heart rather than go out and cause a scandal.
38. If you want to cause him confusion, give him a choice.
39. A bad work man blames his tools.
40. O departing one leaves behind good deed.
41. It early pricks that will be a thorn.
42. Every knot has someone to undo it.
43. As you make your bed, so you must lie on it.
44. A little spark can kindle a great fire.
45. A man's shirt does not change the colour of his skin.
46. A narrow place can contain a thousand friends.
47. A small house is enough room for a thousand friends.
48. A virgin may travel alone at midnight and be safe and a purse of gold dropped in the road at midnight will never be stolen.
49. All ways lead to the mill.
50. An aleppine can sell even a dried donkey skin.
51. An ignorant person is simply an enemy to himself.
52. Be not water, talking the tint of all colours.
53. Birth is the massage of death.
54. Dwell not upon thy weariness, thy strength shall be according to the measure of thy desire.

55. Even paradise is no fun without people.
56. Girl, do not exult in thy wedding dress, see how much trouble lurks behind it.
57. If you conduct yourself properly, see how much trouble lurks behind it.
58. In every village, there is there is a path that leads to the mill.
59. It is better to deal with the devil we know than the devil we don't know.
60. It is an easy thing to find a stuff to beat a dog.
61. Kiss any arm you cannot break, and pray to god to break it.
62. Marry a girl of a good family though she be seated on a mat, very poor.
63. No one cries for losing money but the one who earned the money, no one cries for losing the child but his mother.
64. Stone dead hath no fellow.
65. The cloth of the shame does not warm and if it does, it does so only briefly.
66. The land is cultivated by its own oxen.
67. The Mouse fell from the ceiling, and the Cat cried Allah.
68. The person who deals in camels should make the door high.
69. The Zawan of your own country is better than the wheat of strangers.
70. When you are dead, your sister's tears will dry as time goes on, your widows tears will cease in another's arm, but your mother will mourn you until she dies.
71. When your neighbour shave, you start to wet you cheeks.
72. Writing is the mother of eloquence and the father of artists.

Tao sayings

1. What is in the end to be thrown down, begin by being first set on high?
2. We shape clay into a pot, but it is the emptiness inside that hold whatever we want.
3. Be a spot on the ground where nothing is growing where something might be planted, a seed, from the absolute.

Thailand

1. Bald people can always find a comb.
2. Life is so short we must move very slowly.
3. With one stump you can't make good fire.
4. Wait until the tree has fallen before you jump over it.
5. At high tide the Fish eats ants; at low tide the ants eat fish.
6. Bad seven times, good seven times.
7. To apply gold leaf to the leaf, to the back of a Buddha image.
8. Buddhist holy days do not take place only once.
9. A dog jealously guarding a fishbone.
10. Don't catch fish with both hands.
11. Forget the sour for the sweet.
12. Escape from the tiger, meet the crocodile.
13. The tiger hiding its claws.
14. Excessive greed lost windfall.
15. Firing one shot obtaining two birds.
16. The authority of those who teach is often an obstacle to those who want to learn.
17. The best teacher is the one who makes himself progressively unnecessary.
18. When you don't dance well, you blame it on the flute and the drum.
19. Ten cowries shells near at hand.
20. Don't turn over the rubbish to look for a centipede.
21. To cut the bamboo stem before you see the water.
22. To get something, one must sacrifice something.
23. To die to spite the graveyard.
24. To tale face powder to sell ton palace ladies.
25. When you enter a town where people wink, wink as they do.
26. Don't beat yourself before the fever arrives.

27. Slowly, slowly, you will get a fine knife.
28. The dog doesn't shit where there is no rubbish.
29. If you have twenty five satang, save it until you make it up to a habit.
30. Listen with one ear and keep the other ear.
31. To talk like someone cracking shells.
32. It's hard to bend an old tree.
33. To ride an elephant to catch a grass hopper.
34. Windows have ears, doors have holes.
35. Even a four-legged animal can stumble.
36. To cry like a turtle being grilled.
37. Little birds build nests according to their size.
38. To apply gold leaf to the back of a Buddha image.
39. Don't hasten to ripen before being nearly ripe first.
40. If you play with a dog, the dog will lick your mouth.
41. Sweet mouth, sour bottom.
42. In hot water the fish lives, in cold water the fish dies.
43. He has honey in the mouth and razor at the girdle.
44. Flies are easier caught with honey than with vinegar.
45. Look at the direction of the wind.
46. The worth of a thing is best known by the want of it.
47. We never miss the water until the well runs dry.
48. Don't break the handle of a knife with your knee.
49. Who removes the stones, bruised their fingers.
50. Cover one whole dead elephant with a lotus leaf.
51. What is done by night appears by day.
52. The charm at the tip of a ladle, husband will love you to death.
53. The way to a man's heart is through his stomach.
54. Us shrimps to bait a perch.

55. Many lawyers many cases.
56. If you talk, you will only get a small sum of money.
57. If you love your cow, tie it up; if you love your child beat him.

Tunisia

1. A bull wants to impregnate a cow, and it came back a foetus.
2. After I saw what my mother did, I will never trust a widow.
3. Because he has so many trades, he is unemployed.
4. He ate one fig and he thought the autumn had come.
5. He who is covered with other people's clothes is naked.
6. He who spends a night with a chicken will cackle in the morning.
7. He who wants to be famous will have many sleepless nights.
8. Hit him with a bean, he will break.
9. How lovely is the sun after rain, and how lovely is laughter after sorrow.
10. If he gives you a rope, tie him with it.
11. If my belly is of glass, I will fill it with bread and chicken, if it is closed cellar, I will fill it with cockroaches.
12. If someone hit you with a stone, hit him bread, your bread will return to you and his stone will return to him.
13. If the full moon loves you, why worry about the stars.
14. If the tail of the dog can save me, I don't care about its stench.
15. If there is any profit in partnership, two will share a woman.
16. If you are ugly, be winsome.
17. If your friend is honey, don't lick him thoroughly.
18. No one will say "my father is inconsistent".
19. Everyone will say "he is a man of advice and wisdom".

20. One hundred alcoholics are better than one gambler.
21. Pretend that you are crazy, you will live.
22. The anger of a woman is mighty and the devil's trickery weak.
23. The bald woman boasts of her sister's hair.
24. The multitude is stronger than the king.
25. The only difference between the cucumber and water is the moving of the teeth.
26. There is no blindness but the blindness of the heart.
27. They asked the female cat why her kittens were of different colours, she said she is embarrassed to say no.
28. The asked the mule who is father was.
29. They ate our food, and forgot our names.
30. We praised the bride, and she was found pregnant.
31. Who came back from the grave and told the story.
32. You should have done it on the wedding night, you fool.

Turkey

1. A heart in love with beauty never grows old.
2. Do not speak sweet words when your deeds are of stone.
3. The cheese vessels will not sail merely by words.
4. There are many words that are like salted jam.

Tywan

1. A bird has a nest, man has home.
2. A good person has many friends; a good Horse has a master.
3. A spoken word, carved wood.
4. Even though he misses his duck, he will not miss his lake.
5. Even though his stomach is satiated, his eye will not be satiated.
6. Even though it is black, the raven loves its young.
7. Livestock become acquainted by neighing to one another, people become.
8. Man grow up, felt wears out.
9. Nutcrackers crack cedar seeds, monk crack rosary beats.
10. Small laziness leads to big laziness.
11. The camel station grows old, the camel foal grows up.
12. The dog orders its tail.
13. The horn that came out last will pass the ear that came out first.
14. The hurrying mouse falls into milk.
15. The mountain makes the horse suffer, anger makes oneself suffer.
16. The old horse will not mistake the road.
17. There is no fish in well-water; there is no leaf on dry wood.
18. Today's lung is better than tomorrow's fat.
19. Tumbleweed enters the mouth of the lying camel.
20. When hitting the horn of a single cow, the horn of a thousand Cows hurt.
21. When there is killing weather, the dogs grow fat.
22. When water reaches up to the nose, the calf is a swimmer.
23. Without seeing the water, do not take off your boots.

24. Without father-half orphan, without mother complete orphan.
25. Without wind, the ears of the grass do not move.

Uganda

1. Caution is not cowardice, even the Ants march armed.
2. The hunter in pursuit of an Elephant does not stop to throw stones at Birds.
3. The husband is always the last to know.
4. The person who has not travelled widely thinks his or her mother is the best cook.
5. He, who hunts two Rats, catches none.
6. A roaring Lion kills no game.
7. A strawberry blossom will moisten dry bread.
8. If you hear a madman talking, wait for a minute you will hear what makes people think he is mad.
9. A fool is always right in his own eyes – no wonder he is a fool.
10. The prosperity of the tree is the well-being of the Birds.
11. If your mouth turns into a knife, it will cut off your lips.
12. An old man who by himself carries one load on the head and another in his hand must have played away his youth.
13. No one drinks hot paper soup in a hurry.
14. There is no need to hurry in licking of the finger because it will not be put away on the rafter.
15. The heart of a man and the bottom of the sea are unfathomable.
16. Do not call the forest that shelters you a jungle.
17. One must first praise the farmer for a job well done before asking him for a yam.
18. Do not tell the man that is carrying that he stinks.
19. All of us cannot sleep and place our heads in the same direction.
20. The Cock that is drunk is yet to meet the Hawk that is irate.

21. When the Cock is drunk he forgets about the Hawk.
22. The one who over fears, is the one who meets with hardships.
23. It takes a village to raise a child.
24. He, who learns, teaches.
25. When the door is opened, the mouth is opened.
26. The fool speaks, the wise listens
27. After a fool deed, comes remorse.
28. The king, who surround himself with good counsellors has good reign.
29. One cannot run away from his behind.
30. A man, who knows the use of proverbs, reconciles difficulties.
31. Knowledge is not the main thing, but good deeds are.
32. The child that washes his hands will get to eat with elders.

Ukraine

1. A Crow will never be falcon.
2. A friendly word is better than a heavy cake.
3. You can burn down a house, but can you hide the smoke?
4. A hungry Wolf is stronger than a satisfied Dog.
5. A woman's beauty cannot warm a winter's night.
6. Black souls wear white shirts.
7. Borrowed bread lies heavy on the stomach.
8. Deficiencies come by kilo and go by the gram.
9. Drink a glass of wine after your soup and you will be stealing a rubble from the doctor.
10. Drunkards know no danger.
11. Every disadvantage has its advantage.
12. Fire begins with spark.
13. Flies will no land on the boiling pot.
14. Fools love not the wise, drunkards love not the sober.
15. God is looking for those who come to him.
16. God sits on high and sees far.
17. He is guilty who is not at home.
18. He who licks knives will soon cut his tongue.
19. If the devil is powerless, send him a woman.
20. If you marry a young woman, make sure your friends stay outside.
21. Keep fire away from straw.
22. Love tells us many things that are not so.

Vietnam

1. Eating is much but accommodating but little.
2. Eating as in the north, clothing as in the south.
3. You eat slowly, that is good for the stomach, you plough deeply, and that is good fields.
4. When having party, go first, when walking in the water, go after.
5. One Worm may damage the whole cooking soup.
6. Eating and sitting without labour.
7. Eating nothing but saying yes.
8. Try to seize the bowel of rice but forget the whole table of food.
9. One piece of food while hungry equals a big box of food while full..
10. The husband eats hamburger, the wife eats spring roll.
11. Eat as strong as Elephant.
12. Eat as small as a Cat.
13. Looks as Monkey eats ginger.
14. The good leaves protect the Worm-out leaves.
15. A chilli is hot, all women are jealous.
16. Good wine must drink together with friends.
17. We fence (or protect) the tree that gives us fruits.
18. When eating chew well, think before speaking.
19. When eating choose the place, when playing choose your friends.
20. Eat the plum (given as a gift) but give back a peach.
21. It's better to salty food and speak the truth than eat vegetarian and tell lies.
22. When you eat, its vegetables, when you are sick it's a medicine.
23. Pay first and then get what you have paid for.

24. The student tried to steal the cooking Fish. The teacher found out. The student says Oh forgive me, I just opened the Fish container. * If you were a bit later, I would have taken the whole Fish container.
25. When you eat, check the pots and pans, when you sit, check the direction.
26. Eating as flying Dragon, speaking as climbing Dragon and working as a vomiting Cat.
27. Hunger finds no fault with cookery.
28. Though he eats alone, he calls the whole village to help launch his boat.
29. Because the caterpillar exists, there exists also a Bird to eat it.
30. Don't spurn cold rice, hunger helps you eat even food that has gone bad.
31. Eaten bread is soon forgotten.
32. Many dishes make many diseases.
33. Eat to see the bowel, go to see the way.
34. If you won't work, you shall not eat.
35. Stolen food is the best.
36. However sharp it is, the knife will never cut its own handle.
37. Heave rewards and reprimands. Heaven never reprimands those who are eating.
38. When eating fruits, remember those who planted the tree, when drinking clear water, remember who dug the well.
39. When Cats steals a piece of meat, we chase it, but when a Tiger takes a Pig we stare wide-eyed and say nothing.
40. Feeding boys without teaching them, we raise asses; feeding girls without teaching them we raise Pigs.

41. The educated man precedes the farmer, but when the rice begins to run short, it's the farmer who comes first.
42. The hard labour and continuing effort in sharpening or moulding a piece of iron will one day become a precious and well defined piece of metal.

Virgin Islander

1. "Come see me" and "come live with me" are two different things.
2. A new broom sweeps clean, but an old broom knows the corners.
3. An empty sac can't stand up, full sack cannot bend.
4. If you think your bundle of dirty clothes is too heavy try picking your neighbour.
5. Never pick up what you didn't put down.
6. No matter how fast moonlight runs daylight catches up.
7. The bucket goes down the well everyday….some say it won't come up again.
8. Willing is a good man, but abler is a better one.
9. You can lock your door from a thief, but not from a damned liar.

Walloon

1. A tree falls the way it cleans.
2. Beauty is not much what you see as what you dream.
3. Better warn than be warned.
4. Do what you want, but make sure you are first.
5. Don't make use of another's mouth unless it has been leant to you.
6. Fat gees don't fly far.
7. He started with nothing and still he has just his begging bags.
8. He, who keeps his mouth shut, dies without confession.
9. In dark weather the devil is in the air.
10. The best ointment comes in small boxes.
11. The chemist doesn't smell his own medicine.
12. The more the Billy Goat stinks, the more the nanny Goat loves him.
13. The tail is always the most difficult part to skin.
14. Three hairs are quickly combed.
15. When two poor men help each other, God laughs.
16. White flowers are not to be found in a coal sack.
17. You only know saints by their miracle.

Welsh

1. A warm January, a cold May.
2. A watched clock never tell time.
3. A watched pot never boils.
4. A wife's advice is not worth much, but woe to the husband who refuses to take it.
5. A wilful thought has no excuse and deserve no pardon.
6. A wilful man must have his way.
7. Adversity and loss make a man wise.
8. Adversity brings knowledge, and knowledge wisdom.
9. Adversity comes with instruction in his hand.
10. Be honourable yourself if you wish to associate with honourable people.
11. Have a Horse of your own and then you may borrow another.
12. He understands badly who listens badly.
13. If every fool wore a crown, we should all be kings.
14. If every man would sweep his own door step the city would soon be clean.
15. If you would get ahead, be a bridge.
16. Man's mind is a watch that needs winding daily.
17. Nothing is as clean as Fish.
18. Of a complement only a third is meant.
19. Old age is a hundred disorders.
20. Old age will not come alone.
21. Reason is the wise man's guide, example the fools.
22. The advice of the age will not mislead you.
23. The best candle is understanding.
24. Three remedies of physician of myddfal: water, honey, and labour.
25. Three things it is the best to avoid; strange dogs, flood and a man who think he is wise.
26. Without perseverance talent is a barren bed.

27. Your hand is never the worse for doing its own work.
28. Bad news goes about in clogs, good news in stocking feet.
29. He that would be a leader must be a bridge.
30. Perfect love sometimes does not come until grandchildren are born.
31. Three things give us hardy strength; sleeping on hairy mattress, breathing cold air, and eating dry food.
32. Your hand is never the worse foe doing its own work.
33. People aren't good unless others are made better by them.
34. Conscience is the nest where all good is hatched.

Yiddish

1. A child's tear rends the heavens.
2. A chip on the shoulder indicates wood higher up.
3. A dog without teeth will also attack a bone.
4. A fool is his own informer.
5. A fool says what he knows and a wise man knows what he says.
6. A fool shows his annoyance at once, but a prudent man overlooks an insult.
7. A fool who can keep silent is counted among the wise.
8. A golden key will open every lock.
9. A half truth is a whole lie.
10. A jest is half a truth.
11. A joke driven too far brings home hate.
12. A man cannot jump over his own shadow.
13. A man cannot spin and reel at the same time.
14. A man comes from dust and in the dust he will end- and in the meantime it is good to drink a sip of vodka.
15. A man is not honest simply because he never had a chance to steal.
16. A man is not old until his regrets take the place of his dreams.
17. A man should live if only to satisfy his curiosity.
18. A penny is a lot of money... if you haven't got a penny.
19. A penny is sometimes better spent than spared.
20. A penny saved is a penny earned.
21. A rich man who is stingy is the worst pauper.
22. A rich man's foolish sayings pass for wise ones.
23. A Snake deserves no pity.
24. A table is not blessed if it has fed no scholars.

25. A wise man hears one word and understands two.
26. After nine month the secret comes out.
27. All signs are misleading.
28. Better ask ten times than go astray once.
29. Beware of still waters, a still dog, and a still enemy.
30. Bygones troubles are good to tell.
31. Change nothing and you will get a lot of customers.
32. Charity and pride have different aims, yet both feed the poor.
33. Charity covers a multiple of sins.
34. Charm is more than beauty.
35. Dear God, you do such wonderful things for complete strangers, why not for me.
36. Don't throw a stone into a well from wonderful things for complete strangers, why not for me.
37. Don't throw a stone into a well from which you have drunk.
38. Don't throw away the old bucket until you know whether the new one hold water.
39. Every seller praises his wares.
40. Everyone is kneaded out of the same dough but not in the same oven.
41. Flattery makes a friend and truth makes enemies.
42. Flattery sits in the parlour when plain dealing is the kicked out of doors.
43. Flattery will get you nowhere.
44. Fleas are not lobster.
45. God created a word full of little worlds.
46. God made man because he loves stories.
47. Gold's father is dirt, yet it regards itself as noble.
48. Golden dishes will never turn black.

49. Golden dreams make men wake hungry.
50. Have you gotten up early; you wouldn't have needed to stay up late.
51. He falsifies who renders a verse just as it looks.
52. He that can't endure the bad will not live to see the good.
53. He that cannot ask cannot live.
54. He that cannot obey cannot command.
55. He that cannot pay let him pray.
56. He that comes for the inheritance is often made to pay for the funeral.
57. Hell shared with a sage is better than paradise with a fool.
58. If a link is broken, the whole chain breaks.
59. If a man is destined to drown, he will drown even in a spoonful of water.
60. If all pulled in one direction, the world would keel over.
61. Each one sweeps before his own door, the whole street is clean.
62. If the people could hire other people to die for them, the poor make wonderful living.
63. If Saint Paul's day be fair and clear, it will betide a happy year.
64. If things are not as you wish, wish them as they are.
65. If we did not flatter ourselves, nobody else could.
66. If you ever needed a helping hand you will find one at the end of your arm.
67. If you want your dreams to come true, don't sleep.
68. Interest on debts grows without rain.
69. Love tastes sweet, but only with bread.
70. Make new friends, but don't forget the old ones.

71. Make no more haste than good speed.
72. Make sure to send a lazy man for the Angel of death.
73. Many complain of their looks, but none of their brains.
74. Measure the corns of others with your own bushel.
75. Money buys everything but good sense.
76. Money does not grow on trees.
77. Not everyone who sits in the seat of honour is master.
78. One good deed has many claimants.
79. One good for wit is worth two after wit.
80. One person enjoys a piece of hard cheese, a second a spun out of prayer chant, and a third a door of street.
81. Parents can give everything but common sense.
82. Prayers go up and blessings come down.
83. Protest long enough that you are right, and you will be wrong.
84. Provide the worst; the best can take care of itself.
85. Seek advice but use your own common sense.
86. Seek and ye shall find.
87. Send a fool to close the shutters and he will close them all over town.
88. Send a fool to the market and a fool he will return.
89. Show a Dog a finger and he wants the whole hand.
90. Show her the rudder but don't steer her boat.
91. Silence is also speech.
92. Sleep faster, we need the pillows.
93. Talk too much, and you talk about yourself.
94. Talking comes by nature, silence by wisdom.
95. The complete fool is half prophet.

96. The entire world rests on the tip of the tongue.
97. The girl who can't dance says the band can't play.
98. The glacier didn't freeze overnight.
99. The nearer to the synagogue, the faster from God.
100. The schlemiel on his back and bruises his nose.
101. The soldiers' fights and the kings are heroes.
102. The truly rich ones are those who enjoy what they have.
103. The wheel turns around.
104. The wise man, even when he holds his tongue, says more than the fool when he speaks.
105. Time and words cannot be recalled, even if it was only yesterday.
106. To every answer you can find a new question.
107. Tomorrow your Horse may be lame.
108. Trouble is the man, what rust is to iron.
109. Truth is the safest liar.
110. Truth never dies, but lives a wretched life.
111. We are all schlemiels.
112. Weeping makes the heart grow lighter.
113. What you save is, later, like something found.
114. When a thief kisses you, count your teeth.
115. When fortunes calls, offer her a chair.
116. When luck joins in the game, cleverness scores double.
117. When one must, one can.
118. When the light is crooked, the shadow is crooked.
119. With time, even a Bear can learn to dance.
120. Words should be weighted, not counted.
121. Words show the wit of a man, but actions his meaning.
122. Worries go better with soup than without.

123. You buy yourself an enemy when you lend man money.
124. You can throw a Cat whoever you want; it always falls on its feet.
125. You cannot chew with somebody else's teeth.
126. You cannot measure the whole world with your own yardstick.
127. Your health comes first; you can always hang yourself later.
128. Your neighbour's apples are the sweetest.
129. Your pot broken seems better than my whole one.

Yoddish

1. A man is not honest simply because he never had a chance to steal.
2. A table is not blessed if it has fed no scholars.
3. A wise men hears one word and understands two.
4. All things grow with time except grief.
5. An angry man is no fit to pray.
6. An old maid who marries becomes a young wife.
7. As we live, we learn.
8. Don't judge a man by the words of his mother; listen to the comments of his neighbours.
9. Dying young is a boon in old age.
10. He is a fool who looks for a notch in saw.
11. How many will listen to the truth when you tell them.
12. If the rich would hire other people to die for them, the poor could make a wonderful living.
13. It was hard for Satan alone to mislead the world, so he appointed rabbis in different localities.
14. Look down if you would know how high you stand.
15. Love is sweet, but taste best with bread.
16. Measure the corn of the others with your own bushel.
17. Not the mouse is a thief, but the hole in the wall
18. Parents can give a dowry, but not good luck.
19. Poverty is no disgrace, but no honour either.
20. Sooner ask a man for his life, than for his money.
21. The constant friend is never welcome.
22. The devil comes to us in our hour of darkness, but we do not have to let him in. and we do not have to listen either.
23. The inner keeper loves the drunkard, but not for a son in law.

24. The longest road in the world is the one that leads to the pocket.
25. The truth is not always what we want to hear.
26. The wise man, even when he holds his tongue, says more than a fool when he speaks.
27. The wool seller knows the buyer.
28. Time and words can't be recalled, even if it was only yesterday.
29. Tomorrow your horse may be lame.
30. When a man has luck. Even his Ox calves.
31. When the Ox stumbles, all wet their knives.
32. When you get to the top, don't look back.
33. Your health comes first; you can always hang yourself later.
34. Your neighbour's apples are the sweets.

Zambian

1. A belching toad portends rain.
2. A fat woman warms even the coldest night.
3. A man with a cross eye shall be put to the torch.
4. A Monkey that pilfers from a window's must not be admonished.
5. A riddle made by god has no solution.
6. A strong bull is seen by its scars.
7. A tender Bamboo cannot be eagerly desired for building.
8. A wild Dog is best eaten when clubbed to death.
9. A woman without teeth shall be left to the lions.
10. An old poacher makes the best gamekeeper.
11. Beat your wife regularly, if you don't know why, she will.
12. Do not look at a visitor's face but at his stomach.
13. He who has a fever is not shown to the fire.
14. He, who listened to the woman, suffered famine at harvest time.
15. He, who paddles two canoes, sinks.
16. I am because we are; we are because I am.
17. If you are ugly, learn how to dance.
18. If you have no teeth, do not break the clay cooking pot.
19. It is better to walk than curse the road.
20. It is inevitable that two thighs will rub against each other.
21. Jump over a log but not over your neighbour's world.
22. Lies have short legs.
23. Many are the eyes of the person whose spouse commits adultery.
24. One who enters a forest does not listen to the breaking of the twigs in the brush.

25. The king lives way up where the stench of the poor cannot reach him.
26. The one who has eaten cannot swim with the Shark that is hungry.
27. Things that are stolen will really never make you rich.
28. To get rid of anger, first weed out the bitter roots.
29. To give is to put.
30. Treat the days well and they will treat you well.
31. When you run alone, you run fast, when you run together, you run far.
32. When you show the moon to the child, it sees only your finger.
33. When your luck deserts you, even cold food burns.
34. When God cooks there's no smoke.
35. You can trust your brother, your father, your mother, but never your wife / (husband).
36. You have to look after wealth, but knowledge looks after you.
37. You learn a lot about a man by his behaviour when hungry.
38. Your feet will take you away from home, but your stomach will always bring you back.

ZEN

1. Do not seek the truth; only, cease to cherish your opinion.
2. If you understand, things are just as they are, if you don't understand, things are just as they are.
3. In the landscape of spring, there is neither better nor worse. The flowering branches grow naturally, some long, some short.
4. It takes wise men to learn from his mistakes, but even wiser man to learn from others.
5. Knock on the sky and listen to the sound.
6. The ten thousand questions are one question. If you cut through the one question, then the ten thousand questions disappear.
7. The tighter you squeeze the less you have.
8. The ways to the one are as many as lives of men.
9. Though the Bamboo forest is dense, water flows through freely.
10. To do certain kind of thing, you have to be a certain kind of person.
11. To follow the path, look to the master, follow the master, walk with the master, see through the master, become the master.
12. To know that there is nothing to know, and to grieve that it is difficult to communicate this "to others-this is the life of Zen.
13. When the pupil is ready to learn, a teacher will appear.
14. When you reach to the top, keep climbing.
15. Why do you ask questions? If you already knew the flame was fire then the meal was cooked a long time ago.
16. I only knew a snowflake cannot exist in the storm fire.
17. A weed is a plant whose virtues are only waiting to be discovered.

18. Women may spend their whole lives looking for true love. If you wish for me true love, learn to love yourself.
19. If you do not wait for fulfilment, but brace yourself for failure.
20. Zen students must learn to waste time conscientiously.
21. No yesterday, no tomorrow and no today.
22. If the problem has a solution, worrying is pointless; in the end the problem will be solved. If the problem has no solution, there is no reason to worry, because it cannot be solved.

Zimbabwe

1. Whoever ploughs with a team of donkey must have patience.
2. We will be grateful to flowers only if they have born fruits.
3. The more help in the cornfield the smaller the harvest.
4. The Monkey does not see his own hind backside, he sees his neighbours.
5. If your mouth were a knife it would cut off your lips.
6. If you can walk you can dance, if you can talk you can sing.
7. Every Elephant has to carry its own trunk around.
8. Blood is sweat of heroes
9. Annoy your doctor and sickness come laughing.
10. A woman is attractive when she is somebody else's wife.
11. An Elephant's tusks are never too heavy for it.
12. Water that can be spoilt can also be purified.
13. A naughty cripple will dance while balancing by the wall.
14. Only tease the handicapped after death.
15. Big mountains pass on the mist to each other.
16. It's not pride, when those live in the mountain ask those on the ground for cornerstones.
17. To climb a mountain you must go up round the mountain.
18. Behind the prayer there is no prayer.
19. No matter how thorough a Crow bathes, it is black.
20. A wasp may be crooked, but it has the motivation.
21. A prince is a slave when far from his kingdom.
22. A big group of Mice won't leave traces.

23. A small Bird may fend for food in the husk whilst its heart is in the grain.
24. The wearing out of an animal hide is as if it never had meat.
25. After leaving a Cattle kraal, a white grub thinks itself a Cow too.
26. A poor person won't kill an animal that has leather.
27. A Baboon may be ugly but it won't eat a carcass.
28. Something killed it an Owl can't die because of the wind.

Zimbabwe (Shona Proverbs)

1. Innocent Dogs chew up leather mats.
2. Impossibility is impossibility, a cough cannot abort pregnancy.
3. The power of Fish is in the water.
4. One finger can't squeeze a flea.
5. If the gods give you a wound, they have allowed flies to eat you.
6. Anything knew is under your feet.
7. Lone planer burnt his own blanket.
8. During courtship a man humbles himself, the raises his head after winning the woman's heart.
9. A small flame burnt huge logs down.
10. Running is not getting there.
11. The heart is like a tree, it grows where it wishes.
12. The only place that is far for a Hyena is the place that has no food.
13. He who has skin has meat, it's better than having bone.
14. He who weeps shed tears.
15. He who warns you is a friend.
16. A hill is steep for those who live far off, those who live near, play running uphill and downhill.
17. You have no power on what does not belong to you.
18. Only what you have eaten is surely yours, what you haven't is owed to the king.
19. What grows withers away, an old Baboon's head is deformed into the shape.
20. A sin against the gods is not repaid the day it is committed.
21. You would know your grandmother after being told.
22. "If I had known" cannot guide you.

23. The boss is always the boss. A big Bird can't perch on grass leaves.
24. A Goat will only give birth in front of people to be protected from Dogs.
25. A fig may be appetizing form outside but it's full of Ants inside.
26. A mature Baboon who humbles himself will be feared, respected by little ones.
27. Kind-hearted can backfire.
28. Any beautiful woman who is not a thief must be a witch.
29. Bitter medicine truly heals.
30. To eat nursing mother's food, you must cuddle her baby first.
31. Thanking a consignment of unknown origin equals thanking the delivery boy.
32. Panic over trivia exposes guilt.
33. Only dread a Hyena if you have fat smeared all over your body.
34. A huge Snake will not bite itself.
35. One who is running out of ideas will search for a bow in pots.
36. Inherit after seeing success of other inheritance.
37. A Bee must suck from only one flower because the flower of the world are unnumbered.
38. Cross a big lake once, by the time you come back all Crocodiles will be alert.
39. When a drum begins to play a higher pitch it's about to break.
40. A fool who asks is good.
41. An offer comes from where another comes.

Zulu (South Africa)

1. You can learn wisdom at your grandfather's feet or at the end of a sick.
2. A walking man builds no kraal.
3. You cannot know the good within yourself if you cannot see it in others.
4. When you bite indiscriminately, you end up eating your own tail.
5. The Lion is a beautiful animal, when seen at a distance.
6. The bones must be thrown in three different places before the message must be accepted.
7. Guessing breeds suspicion.
8. Even immortals are immune to fate.
9. You cannot fight on evil disease with sweet medicine.
10. Old age doesn't announce itself at the gate of the kraal.
11. Almost doesn't fill a bowl.
12. Even the most beautiful flowers withers in time.
13. The sun never set that there has not been fresh news.
14. Do not speak of a rhinoceros if there no tree nearby.
15. The world is a harsh place.
16. This, too, shall pass.
17. The seed wait for its garden or ground where it will be sown.
18. Abundance does not spread. Famine does.
19. No stake ever grew old with the bark on.
20. Almost is not eaten.
21. He was kicked by a Horse in the chest.
22. A way forward is asked from those who are in front.
23. The mouth is a tail to switch away flies.
24. A fault confessed is half redressed.

www.ingramcontent.com/pod-product-compliance
Lightning Source LLC
LaVergne TN
LVHW051623080426
835511LV00016B/2143